WEATHER IN YOUR LIFE

Weather in Your Life

Louis J. Battan

The University of Arizona

W. H. Freeman and Company
San Francisco

Project Editor: Judith Wilson
Designer: Sharon Helen Smith
Production Coordinator: William Murdock
Illustration Coordinator: Richard Quiñones
Artist: John Cordes
Compositor: Graphic Typesetting Service
Printer and Binder: The Maple-Vail Book Manufacturing Group

Credits for chapter-opening photographs: Chapter 1, © Laurence Cameron/Jeroboam, Inc. Chapter 2, *New York Journal American,* Wide World Photos. Chapter 3, Photo by Joseph Demmer. Courtesy of NSSL/NOAA. Chapter 4, © Emilio Mercado/ Jeroboam, Inc. Chapter 5, Courtesy of National Earth Satellite Service/NOAA. Chapter 6, Photo by Noel M. Klein, courtesy of NOAA. Chapter 7, © Evan Johnson/Jeroboam, Inc. Chapter 8, Courtesy of Chessie System. Chapter 9, © Werner Hiebel/ Alphapress/Jeroboam, Inc. Chapter 10, Photo by W.E. Kesler, courtesy of *St. Louis Post-Dispatch.* Chapter 11, © Kent Reno/ Jeroboam, Inc. Chapter 12, © Bill Owens/Jeroboam, Inc. Chapter 13, Courtesy of Kunsthistorisches Museum, Vienna.

Library of Congress Cataloging in Publication Data

Battan, Louis J.
    Weather in your life.

    Bibliography: p.
    Includes index.
    1. Weather—Popular works. 2. Climatology—Popular
works. I. Title.
QC981.2.B37   1983   551.6   82-20925
ISBN 0-7167-1436-1
ISBN 0-7167-1437-X (pbk.)

Printed in the United States of America

1 2 3 4 5 6 7 8 9 0 MP 1 0 8 9 8 7 6 5 4 3

CONTENTS

PREFACE

The atmosphere influences life in ways dramatic and subtle—sometimes causing trouble, sometimes giving pleasure. Science has not yet enabled us to master the environment, but a little knowledge enables us to enhance what is best and to avoid the worst. This book examines the weather and its effects and suggests how weather and climate information can be used to make life safer, healthier, and happier.

One of my goals is to introduce individuals with little scientific training to an understanding of the nature of the atmosphere. To this end, I have used familiar English units of measurement and avoided the temptation to include mathematical equations. Because *Weather in Your Life* presents a nontechnical introduction to the basic principles of atmospheric science, it is appropriate both for the general reader and for use as supplementary reading in a variety of undergraduate courses. Students enrolled in environmental studies, meteorology, and climatology should find this book appealing and informative. I hope many readers will acquire an interest that will lead them further.

I wish to thank Arnold Court, a friend of long standing, for his many helpful suggestions, and Robert E. Wanetick for his excellent editing.

Louis J. Battan
October 1982

CHAPTER 1
Introduction

The weather affects the lives of everyone—sometimes in subtle, barely discernible fashions, at other times in dramatic, violent ways that leave permanent scars or even maim and kill. Since the earliest days of life on the earth, humans have cursed the storms and prayed for their cessation. They have pleasured in the warmth of early spring and been thankful for rains that allowed plants to grow and flower.

We still are slaves to the weather gods. Certainly, the shackles are looser than they used to be, but they are not loose enough; as we approach the end of the twentieth century equipped with devices of unbelievable power and sophistication, we still share many of the reactions of our earliest ancestors. We have computers performing tens of millions of operations a second, airplanes flying at twice the speed of sound, space vehicles measuring the properties of planets millions of miles away; yet we still experience the joys of good weather and the beauty of a rainbow, worry about lightning, tolerate blizzards, and suffer the misfortunes of violent storms.

In too many human endeavors, we do not know enough about the weather, and we fail to use the little that we do know. Every year, thousands of people ignore the realities of weather and buy or rent homes in low-lying land along streams and river channels. Then nature comes along in its normal course of events and brings a great deal of rain in a short period of time. The results are floods, human misery, and property losses, sometimes of staggering magnitudes.

Pilots, especially inexperienced ones flying their own airplanes, find it easy to overlook the perils of the weather. As a result, they sometimes find themselves groping blindly through clouds in airplanes not equipped with the necessary instruments. The hazards are amplified when a cloud contains turbulence that can shake and roll an airplane, hail that can hammer the leading surfaces of aluminum or glass, lightning that can burn off radio antennas and temporarily blind the pilot, or high concentrations of very cold water droplets that coat the airplane with layers of ice.

There seems to be a widespread perception among commercial-airline passengers that flying is hazardous. It still is not rare for them to applaud when an airplane has landed safely: Presumably, this is an expression of satisfaction of having survived the flight. Perhaps the newspaper headlines on the infrequent occasion of an airliner crash—or a feeling that human flight is an invasion of the birds' domain and, therefore, not natural— account for the lines at the insurance counters. But let us not forget that the highways claim very many more victims than the airways, and weather is often the cause. Fog on a high-speed turnpike, especially when patchy and thick, can cause the destruction of motor vehicles in bunches. Snow and ice also make roads treacherous; strong winds and flooded roadways pose still other hazards.

The weather has profound effects on agriculture, but do the farmers of the world know as much as they should about those effects and how to deal with them? Of course not! This critical lack of knowledge is not the fault of the farmers alone: They need advice from the weather experts, and they are not getting it.

What would happen if, as the old television commercial used to say, you took your sinuses to Arizona? Although the answer to this is still "up in the air," it is clear that atmospheric conditions influence, sometimes in dramatic ways, certain diseases such as asthma and arthritis. There is also evidence that the weather can have important psychological effects. When hot, dry gusty winds blow down mountain slopes, there is a greater likelihood of emotional traumas and even suicides. These are just a few examples of how the weather plays a role in human affairs.

Almost everyone makes weather-related decisions every day, some as minor as deciding to take an umbrella to work, some of enormous importance in terms of business or the preservation of life. For example, on November 14, 1969, a decision was made to launch *Apollo 12* into an overcast of clouds. The vehicle, with its three astronauts headed for the moon, was struck twice by lightning and disabled seriously—fortunately, only temporarily—and disaster was barely avoided. As another example, in 1978, California farmers decided to allow raisins to dry in the open a few days longer; a storm brought heavy rains, and losses ran into the millions of dollars.

This book contains other examples of how weather and climate information can be of value in making sound decisions of many different kinds. The need for a better understanding of the weather and climate and the importance of an appreciation of the values and limitations of weather forecasts are demonstrated.

This book consists of two parts: The first part gives a description of the atmosphere, weather, and climate and a discussion of weather forecasting and modification. The second part deals with the effects of the atmosphere on a wide spectrum of societal activities.

Scientists are learning to influence the weather; in the future, it may be possible to modify or even control it in a predictable fashion. Until that day comes, we have to deal with it as it is.

A greater knowledge of the factors influencing your life and your occupation should help you to improve them. This small volume can start you down that road. If it stirs your curiosity and leads you to a greater use of weather information, it will have been worth the effort.

CHAPTER 2
Air

The insubstantial substance called air, though crucial to life on earth, is taken for granted by almost everyone. It is always there, but who ever thinks about it—except on polluted days.

Few people realize how much air they breathe. A healthy person fills and empties his lungs about 20,000 times in 24 hours, inhaling about 30 pounds of air. In comparison, a person ingests an average of less than 3 pounds of food and 5 pounds of water in the same period. A person can survive approximately 5 weeks without food and 5 days without water, but only 5 minutes without air.

As Table 2-1 shows, air is actually a mixture of many gases. By volume, dry air is roughly 78 percent nitrogen (N_2) and 21 percent oxygen (O_2), with argon making up most of the remaining 1 percent. When water vapor,

Table 2-1 The Gaseous Composition of the Atmosphere

Dry Air: Constant Gases[1]		Variable Gases[2] (approximate)	
Constituent	Percent by volume	Constituent	Percent by volume
Nitrogen (N_2)	78.08	Water vapor (H_2O)	0–4
Oxygen (O_2)	20.95	Carbon dioxide (CO_2)	0.0340[3]
Argon (Ar)	0.93	Carbon monoxide (CO)	0–0.01
Neon (Ne)	0.0018	Ozone (O_3)	0–0.001
Helium (He)	0.00052	Sulfur dioxide (SO_2)	0–0.0001
Methane (CH_4)	0.00015	Nitrogen dioxide (NO)	0–0.00002
Krypton (Kr)	0.00011		
Hydrogen (H_2)	0.00005		

[1]The composition changes little up to an altitude of about 50 miles.
[2]Gases are variable from time to time and place to place.
[3]The annually averaged concentration of carbon dioxide in 1982 was about 0.0340 and is increasing by about 0.0001 percent per year (see Figure 2-3).

which may represent as much as 4 percent of the volume of air, is present, the other constituents are reduced proportionally.

Atmospheric nitrogen comes mostly from decaying agricultural debris and volcanic eruptions. It is removed from the air largely through biological processes involving vegetation and sea life. In addition, nitrogen is converted to nitrogen oxides by high-temperature combustion in the engines of motor vehicles and airplanes. The concentration of nitrogen in the atmosphere is essentially constant, indicating that inputs are roughly in balance with outputs.

The same can be said about atmospheric oxygen, which is produced largely through the photosynthetic growth of vegetation. In the formation of green matter, the leaves take up carbon dioxide and release oxygen. It is removed from the air by humans and animals, whose lungs take in oxygen and release carbon dioxide. Oxygen is also a component of the water of oceans and lakes; it is consumed as organic matter decays and when it combines with other substances, as in the rusting of iron and steel.

THE OZONE LAYER: AN ULTRAVIOLET SHIELD

Some gaseous constituents of air exist in small, even trace, quantities, but their importance cannot be inferred from the amounts. For example, ozone (O_3), whose molecules consist of three oxygen atoms each, constitutes up to only 0.001 percent of the atmosphere; but without ozone, life on the earth would be different from what it is today. Although ozone is found throughout the lower atmosphere, most of it exists in the stratosphere, the layer between about 40,000 and 160,000 feet above sea level (Figure 2-1). This *ozone layer* is maintained by a complicated series of processes involving the absorption of radiation from the sun.

The sun can be thought of as a huge, gaseous sphere that radiates as if it had a temperature of about 11,000°F. As a consequence of this high temperature, maintained by thermonuclear reactions in the interior, the sun radiates a tremendous quantity of energy, distributed over a wide spectrum of wavelengths (Figure 2-2). This energy is particularly intense at the visible wavelengths. Ultraviolet rays, when sufficiently intense, can cause severe sunburns, skin cancers, and other biological effects. Most ultraviolet radiation does not reach the surface of the earth because it is absorbed by ozone in the stratosphere. In the middle seventies, however, it became evident that certain substances, particularly the Freons used in refrigerators and aerosol spray cans, could cause a reduction in stratospheric ozone. Freon, a trade name for a class of substances called chlorofluoromethanes or fluorocarbons, is wonderful in many respects: Freons are volatile but not flammable, are odorless, and, in the lower atmosphere, are chemically stable and do not react with other substances. Unfortunately, when exposed to ultraviolet radiation, Freon molecules break down

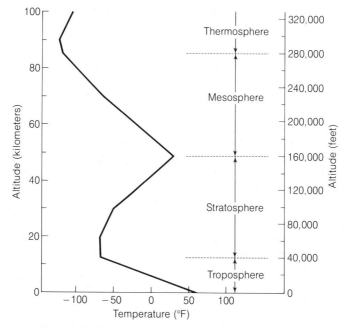

Figure 2-1 Air temperature shown as a function of altitude in the 1976 *U.S. Standard Atmosphere*—an average of many observations. The atmosphere is divided into layers, called "——spheres," according to how the temperature varies with height.

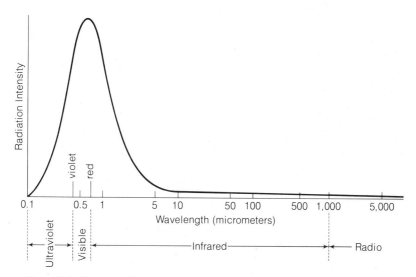

Figure 2-2 A schematic representation of the radiation spectrum of the sun. Note that the horizontal scale is logarithmic. One micrometer (μm) is one-millionth of a meter; i.e., 1 micrometer = 0.000001 meter = 0.00004 inch.

and release chlorine atoms. These, in turn, can react with and reduce the amount of ozone.

Fluorocarbons released at the earth's surface slowly rise, eventually (after 10 to 20 years) reaching the top of the ozone layer, where they are exposed to solar ultraviolet radiation. When this occurs, photochemical reactions slowly but steadily reduce the concentration of ozone. In view of the serious consequences of such a result, the United States government, in 1978, banned the use of fluorocarbons for aerosol spray cans except for certain critical purposes in medical facilities. Freons continue to be used in refrigerators because the annual release of fluorocarbons in such use is relatively small; also, the practical value of refrigeration is greater than that of hair sprays or deodorants. (Other countries, which have accounted for about half of the Freons emitted into the atmosphere, continue to produce and disperse them.)

Other widely used substances, such as nitrogen-based fertilizers and methyl chloroform, which is used as a cleaning agent and solvent, are also suspected of being possible threats to the ozone layer.

No one can be sure at this time if the effects of Freons, fertilizers, and other ozone-threatening substances are as deleterious as some scientists assert. Ozone is naturally highly variable, and small changes are difficult to detect. But in view of the potential seriousness of a substantial depletion of ozone, wisdom dictates a reduction of risks.

CARBON DIOXIDE

Carbon dioxide (CO_2) is a normal, minor constituent of air. Although it represents only about 0.03 percent of the total volume of air, this gas appears to play a major role in the global climate. Carbon dioxide has been getting a great deal of attention in recent years because its concentration in the atmosphere has been increasing. In 1890 it was present in concentrations of about 300 parts per million (ppm); that is, every million parts of air contained 300 parts of carbon dioxide. In 1982 the annual average concentration was about 340 parts per million and increasing by about one part per million per year (Figure 2-3).

Fossil fuels are the chief source of the additional carbon dioxide in the atmosphere: When oil, gas, or coal is burned, carbon dioxide is emitted into the air. Some scientists believe that the clearing of forest lands over the world has also significantly contributed to the increase of carbon dioxide. As mentioned earlier, trees take in carbon dioxide to produce green matter through photosynthesis. Although fewer trees means less carbon dioxide consumed, the evidence suggests that the effect of forest clearing is small compared with that of combustion of fossil fuels.

It is important to know how the concentrations of atmospheric carbon dioxide will change in the future. According to Charles C. Keeling and Robert B. Bacastow, of the University of California at San Diego, if we continue to rely heavily on fossil fuels (particularly coal, which is so abundant in the United States), carbon dioxide concentrations will be about 600 parts per million by the year 2050. Other experts have estimated that this level will be reached within one or two decades of that date.

Carbon dioxide has no effect on solar radiation but readily absorbs infrared radiation emitted by the earth. For this reason, an atmosphere rich in carbon dioxide is sometimes likened to a greenhouse. Water vapor also has little effect on solar radiation but absorbs infrared radiation. If radiation were the only energy transport process at work, it could be concluded that, as atmospheric carbon dioxide increased, the difference between incoming solar radiation and outgoing terrestrial radiation would increase proportionally, leading to an increase in temperature in the lower atmosphere.

In considering the effects of carbon dioxide, however, we must realize that the atmosphere is a complex system and that many factors and processes

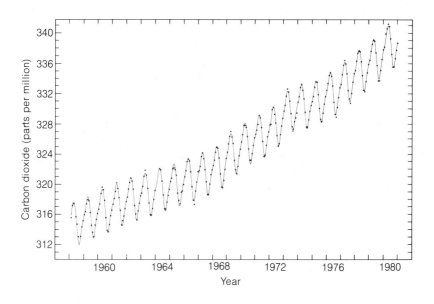

Figure 2-3 Variations of atmospheric carbon dioxide measured at the National Oceanic and Atmospheric Administration (NOAA) baseline station on Mauna Loa, Hawaii. The seasonal periodicities are caused by the seasonal variations in vegetation. Note the progressive increases of the annual averages. (Courtesy of C. D. Keeling and R. B. Bacastow, Scripps Institution of Oceanography.)

are involved in governing the average temperature of the planet. Air and ocean currents transport heat and moisture; constantly changing clouds affect incoming and outgoing radiation. Exchanges of energy and moisture between the atmosphere and the oceans and land, as well as the extent of the ice cover of the earth, significantly influence global temperature.

To deal with this complicated problem, mathematical models that take into account myriad physical and chemical processes must be used (see Chapter 5). Syukuro Manabe and Richard Wetherald, of the National Oceanic and Atmospheric Administration's Geophysical Fluid Dynamics Laboratory at Princeton, have developed such a model. Their calculations indicate that a doubling of carbon dioxide would lead to average warming of about 5°F at the earth's surface with temperature increases perhaps two or three times greater at high latitudes. The consequences could be of enormous significance.

A temperature rise of such a magnitude would be expected to cause changes in the air currents over the earth, the tracks of major storm systems, and the onset time and duration of the summer monsoons that crucially affect food production in Southeast Asia and other places. In the Northern Hemisphere, climatically warm years have been accompanied by below-normal precipitation over the grain belts of the United States and Europe. Many demographers are concerned that, even in optimum circumstances, the world's future populations will be too large to be sustained; a deleterious climate could greviously aggravate the situation.

A global warming would be expected to have many other effects in addition to agricultural ones. For example, it would cause the melting of ice locked in the polar regions—particularly Antarctica. One expert has estimated that a doubling of atmospheric carbon dioxide could lead to enough melting to raise sea level by more than 15 feet. Such an occurrence would cause a geophysical disaster of unprecedented proportions. Cities along coastlines—including many of the world's great cities—would find themselves under water.

The carbon dioxide scenario is a frightening one, but there are many unanswered questions. For example, we need to find out for sure why the carbon dioxide is increasing and obtain better estimates of what is likely to occur in the future. We need to learn more about the consequences of increasing atmospheric carbon dioxide. The Manabe-Wetherald model and similar mathematical models of the earth's atmosphere are impressively informative, but they are not good enough. Even the best models still do not adequately account for the exchanges of energy between air and the underlying land and ocean surfaces. Climatological analyses should reveal whether or not the lower atmosphere of the earth is warming or cooling. In tracking the thermal history of the earth, we must try to discriminate between natural changes and those caused by humans.

If it is shown conclusively that carbon dioxide released by the burning of fossil fuel is leading to significant global warming and that the warming is likely to cause catastrophic results, we should move towards noncarboniferous energy sources as soon as possible. We may have to accept the risks of nuclear energy and accelerate the development of large solar energy systems regardless of the costs.

WATER VAPOR

When water evaporates, its molecules form a gas known as *water vapor.* The atmosphere also contains water in a liquid state, that is, in the form of cloud droplets and raindrops. Ice crystals, snowflakes, and hail are the frozen state of atmospheric water. Weather broadcasters often use the word *moisture* to mean clouds, rain, and snow, but to a meteorologist it represents only invisible water vapor.

Unlike that of most gases in the atmosphere, the presence of water vapor is highly variable. In extremely cold, dry air, water vapor may be barely measurable; in hot, humid air, it may represent as much as 4 percent of the air volume.

The water vapor content of the air often is expressed in terms of *relative humidity,* a quantity that is easily interpreted in terms of everyday activity. For example, if the relative humidity is low—say, 10 percent—wet garments on an outdoor clothesline will dry rapidly, especially on a hot day.

It is no secret that a temperature of 90°F is more comfortable in dry Arizona than in humid Chicago. When the relative humidity is low, body perspiration evaporates quickly and brings cool relief. This fact has led various investigators to formulate scales of comfort that take into account temperature and humidity. We will discuss this further in Chapter 12.

For some purposes, it is necessary to know the precise meaning of relative humidity: It is a ratio, expressed as a percentage, of the actual mass of water vapor in a volume of air to the mass of water vapor that would be present in the same volume if the air were saturated. When air is saturated, its relative humidity is 100 percent; it might be said that saturated air is filled with water vapor.

The ability of air to hold water increases as its temperature increases. For this reason, if the mass of water vapor in the air is constant but the temperature changes, then the relative humidity also changes. This explains why relative humidity usually is lowest in the warm afternoons and highest in the cool early morning hours (Figure 2-4). If there is evaporation of water at the same time that the temperature is increasing, the trend of relative humidity may be either up or down.

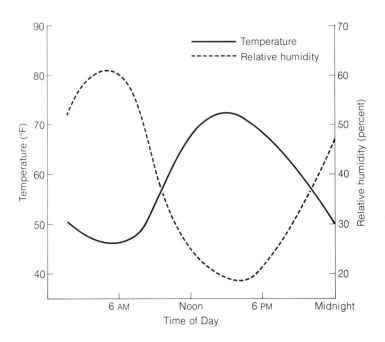

Figure 2-4 Simultaneous diurnal variations of temperature and relative humidity at Tucson, Arizona, on March 17, 1981.

Water vapor enters the atmosphere as a result of evaporation from oceans, lakes, and land masses, and transpiration from plants. The water returns to the surface in the form of rain and snow. Most of it evaporates; the rest seeps into the ground, enters streams and rivers, and flows into lakes and oceans. This sequence of events, illustrated in Figure 2-5, is known as the *hydrologic cycle*.

Water molecules, once evaporated, remain in the atmosphere about 11 days before being precipitated out. This *residence time* of water vapor is much shorter than the residence times of many other atmospheric gases. For example, the residence time of global carbon dioxide is some tens of years; of oxygen, about 3,000 years.

Even with a relatively short residence time of 11 days, most water molecules move great distances from the point of evaporation to the point of precipitation. This fact indicates the fallacy of the idea that the creation of a lake behind a dam is likely to cause more rainfall in the vicinity.

Clouds and precipitation can form only when the relative humidity increases to saturation. In the atmosphere, this happens most often when air rises and cools. The actual process will be discussed later; suffice it to

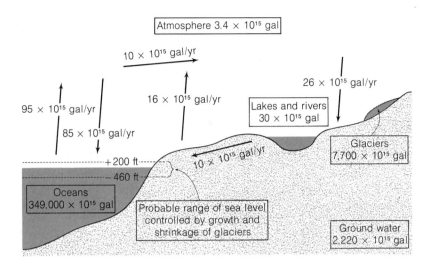

Figure 2-5 The hydrologic cycle: Water moves from the atmosphere to land and oceans by precipitation and returns by evaporation and transpiration. (Based on data by A. L. Bloom, in *The Surface of the Earth,* Prentice-Hall, 1969.)

say, at this point, that when air ascends, clouds and precipitation are likely. When air sinks, clouds and rain are inhibited regardless of how moist the air might be. Prevailing subsidence of air accounts for the existence of arid regions found along low-latitude west-coastal areas, such as California and Mexico, that are immediately downwind of a huge ocean.

AIR POLLUTANTS

An air pollutant is anything that makes air impure or unclean. Any gas, liquid, or solid that is not a normal constituent of the atmosphere, that poses a threat to the health of any living entity, and that causes damage to inanimate objects or reduces the clarity of the atmosphere can be regarded as a pollutant.

The effects of air pollutants on humans sometimes are obvious and dramatic. An example is the air pollution catastrophe that occurred in London in December 1952. Atmospheric conditions were stagnant and stable for about a week, and air pollution concentrations reached high levels, causing the deaths of about 4,000 people. Most of the casualties were people with preexisting lung troubles, who could not stand the additional stress placed upon their lungs.

A great many people suffering pulmonary problems depend on a steady supply of relatively pollutant-free air. When pollution exceeds a certain threshold and does so for a period of days, acute distress is the consequence. Although none was nearly as costly in human life as the London episode, other instances of increased air pollution over a number of days have caused pronounced increases in hospital admissions and deaths. Such was the case at Donora, Pennsylvania, in October 1948.

Fortunately, most people survive periods of even extreme pollution with few obvious aftereffects. However, little is known about the cumulative effects of low levels of various types of pollutants.

Automobile tailpipes emit many gaseous contaminants: nitrogen oxides, carbon monoxide, sulfur dioxide, and hydrocarbons in the form of unburned gasoline. Hydrocarbons and nitrogen oxides react with sunlight to form smog. The main component of smog is a substance that chemists call PAN, an acronym for peroxyacetyl nitrate. On humid days with stagnant air, plenty of cars, and sunshine, the atmosphere becomes hazy with particles

Figure 2-6   Heavy motor vehicle traffic causes air pollution. (Photograph by Gene Daniels, EPA Documerica.)

composed of PAN (Figure 2-6). Such conditions are common in southern California; therefore, so is the occurrence of smog.

Smog occurs often in the Los Angeles basin, but other large urban areas such as Chicago and New York can suffer the same effects when the air is relatively still for several days (Figure 2-7). Such conditions are associated

Figure 2-7   Smog surrounding the Empire State Building in New York. (*New York Journal American*, Wide World Photos.)

with persistent low-level temperature inversions, which trap gases and smokes emitted from tailpipes, smokestacks, and other sources. Most smog victims experience eye irritation and sore throats; fortunately, the problems are temporary and do not lead to serious damage. There is some concern, however, that in extreme, long-lasting episodes, smog may contribute to lung ailments such as cancer. The evidence is conflicting but cannot be ignored.

As noted earlier, ozone occurs naturally in the upper atmosphere, where it is maintained by the absorption of ultraviolet radiation. Ozone is also produced in the lower atmosphere as a result of photochemical reactions that occur when the emissions from the exhaust pipes of motor vehicles are exposed to sunlight. In sufficiently high concentrations, ozone can lead to pulmonary difficulties. According to regulations promulgated by the Environmental Protection Agency in 1979, the standard allowable ozone concentrations at street level should be no greater than 0.12 parts per million. This limit is already exceeded in many of the largest cities in the United States.

Automobiles, improperly ventilated gas-burning indoor heaters, and cigarettes are major sources of another toxic gas—carbon monoxide (CO). It is a colorless, odorless gas that affects its victims without warning. Every year people are killed by running automobile engines in closed garages or having defective exhaust systems that feed carbon monoxide into the passenger compartments. Excessive carbon monoxide released by a floor heater into a closed home also can have fatal results.

Carbon monoxide does its damage by decreasing the transport of oxygen through the body. The CO molecule combines with hemoglobin in the blood to form carboxyhemoglobin (COHb), which cannot combine with oxygen or carry it from the lungs to other body tissues. The quantity of carboxyhemoglobin increases with the concentration of carbon monoxide and the duration of exposure. When a person moves out of a carbon monoxide–rich environment, the blood returns to its original state. Whether or not long-term, low-level exposure to carbon monoxide damages health is still being debated by the experts.

Concentrations of carbon monoxide in the open air are usually below the levels regarded as dangerous. But under stagnant atmospheric conditions in congested, heavily motored urban areas, carbon monoxide concentrations may be high enough to cause dizziness, headaches, and a loss of alertness. Heavy doses have been held to be partly responsible for some automobile accidents. People living in large cities with heavy traffic would be particularly well advised not to smoke. The jolt of concentrated carbon monoxide in each puff of tobacco smoke could be enough to make such people sick or even hasten their passage to the grave.

Nitrogen oxides enter the atmosphere from natural sources and as a result of human activities. Decomposing organic material such as leaves and wood, lightning, high-temperature combustion processes in automobile and airplane engines—all add nitrogen oxides to the atmosphere. In sufficient quantities nitrogen dioxide gas may attack the lungs. It is also a factor in causing eye irritation on polluted days. As a result of complicated chemical processes, nitrogen oxides in the atmosphere can be converted to nitrate compounds that play important roles in the formation of clouds and the acidity of precipitation.

Sulfur dioxide gas is produced by the burning of fossil fuels, such as coal and oil, particularly by electric power plants and smelting and refining operations. Volcanic eruptions are natural sources of large quantities of sulfur dioxide. Chemical reactions in the atmosphere can convert the gas to tiny particles composed of sulfate compounds. For example, typical products of such a process are ammonium sulfate particles, which have a diameter of about 0.000004 inches. Larger, solid grains of blowing soil, smoke, or salt particles from the sea can serve as sites for the deposition of sulfates. As is true of all small particles, they are transported by winds and may leave the atmosphere at places far from the source of the particulate material.

There is widespread suspicion that sulfur dioxide and smoke particles are major contributors to the deadliest atmospheric brews. In sufficiently high concentrations, sulfur dioxide can cause difficulties in the respiratory system. In humid air, sulfur dioxide gas can be converted to minute particles of sulfuric acid. When inhaled, they lodge in the walls of the lungs and impede the takeup of oxygen.

The damage done to *nonliving* things by polluted air is dramatically evident in the old cities of Europe, where the effects of nearby sources of sulfur dioxide are seen in the black, eroded marble of statues and churches (Figure 2-8). In few places is this more obvious than in Venice, where many of the world's greatest works of art and architecture are being slowly destroyed. If satisfactory means are not found to keep sulfuric acid substances off the stone, the inspiring, realistic saints and warriors of Bellini will be washed and eroded to the shape of Henry Moore's modern masterpieces. Civilization needs them all, but as close to the original as possible.

ACID RAIN

Sulfate and nitrate particles are deposited on the earth in a "dry" state. In addition, they serve as the surfaces on which water molecules in the air condense and form cloud droplets. In some circumstances, the droplets

18

A

B

Figure 2-8   A. Deterioration of the Lunetta di Bartolomeo Bon in the Scuola Grande di San Marco in Venice, before the beginning of restoration. (Courtesy of the Superintendent of Architecture of Venice, Italy.)   B. Badly corroded busts of the great philosophers on the front of the Ashmolean Museums in Oxford, England, photographed in 1957. The very soft Headington stone absorbs sulfur dioxide, forming alums that expand under the surface and cause the stone to crumble. The stone of the wall also shows the effects of polluted air. Over the last 25 years, the stone has been replaced by a more resistant stone, and the Clean Air Act of 1956 has brought about reductions of air pollution levels in England. (Courtesy of Richard S. Scorer.)

become parts of raindrops and snowflakes. If the atmosphere contains large concentrations of sulfates or nitrates, rain and snow can have a relatively high degree of acidity.

Chemists measure the acidity of water on a pH (potential hydrogen) scale. A value of 7 is considered neutral, a larger pH is alkaline, and a smaller pH is acidic. A unit change in pH corresponds to a tenfold change in acidity. The widely used term *acid rain* designates precipitation having a pH of less than 5.7.

There have been relatively few reliable, longtime records of the pH of rain and snow in North America. Measurements in western Europe are more extensive. Records from the eastern United States, Canada, and Europe suggest that, since the industrialization of these regions, there have been increases in the acidity of precipitation. The records, however, are not sufficient to prove this point conclusively. But over the recent past, rain and snow over the northeastern United States sometimes have had pH values of 4 or less.

An indirect measure of the acidity of precipitation and of the dry deposition of acidic particles comes from an analysis of the pH of lakes and reservoirs. The average pH of many lakes in the Adirondack Mountains reportedly has dropped from about 6.5 to 4.8 over the last four decades. Many species of fish cannot survive when the pH is at the low end of this range. It has been reported that, because of acidification, about 10,000 lakes in Scandinavia are devoid of fish and an equal number of lakes are threatened.

In most places, the magnitude of the acid rain problem—the cost to society in terms of damage to wildlife, agriculture, paint, and statuary—is only poorly known. The same can be said about the overall costs to further reduce the amounts of sulfur dioxide and nitrogen oxides entering the atmosphere. American industry has spent enormous sums to decrease sulfur dioxide emissions, and it appears that even greater expenditures may be required in the future.

The acid rain problem has important international ramifications because the materials introduced into the atmosphere in one country are sometimes carried into other countries. The highly acidic precipitation in Scandinavia is attributed mostly to sulfur dioxide emissions in the United Kingdom, France, and Germany. Canadians are justifiably concerned about sulfur compounds that are put into the air by industries in the northeastern quadrant of the United States: The sulfur compounds cross the border and acidify the precipitation in Canada.

In one of its analyses, the Environmental Protection Agency estimated that through the end of the century, sulfur oxide emissions into the atmosphere over the United States will remain close to the present levels—about 30 million tons per year (Figure 2-9). However, because of the greater use of coal, annual nitrogen oxide emissions are expected to increase

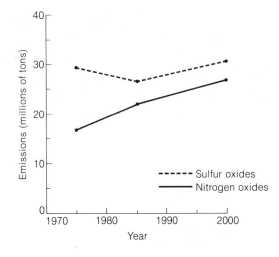

Figure 2-9 Trends in annual emissions of sulfur oxides and nitrogen oxides in the United States, predicted according to the so-called high growth scenario of the Environmental Protection Agency. (From *Environmental Outlook 1980*, EPA.)

from about 17 million tons in 1975 to about 27 million tons by the year 2000. This suggests that the problem of acid precipitation will become more serious in the years to come.

AEROSOLS AND THE CLIMATE

A mixture of particles in air is called an *aerosol,* but often the word is used to represent the particles themselves. Aerosols come from many sources. The larger ones—those having diameters greater than 0.00004 inches—are blown into the air from the land or sea or are the result of combustion or volcanic eruptions. Direct chemical conversions in the atmosphere account for most of the smaller particles, particularly those composed of sulfates.

The number of aerosols in the atmosphere is huge, and there is a steady addition and depletion. The larger particles fall out, while the smaller ones are carried out by rain and snow. Particles in the troposphere—that is, the lower atmosphere (see Figure 2-1)—leave it fairly quickly. The residence times amount to weeks or months depending on the altitudes. On the other hand, tiny solid or liquid aerosols in the stable, generally cloud-free stratosphere can remain there for a year or two.

Powerful volcanic eruptions, such as the Mount Agung explosion in 1963, eject enormous quantities of material into the stratosphere. These include large amounts of sulfur oxides that in the presence of sunlight are converted into sulfate aerosols. They serve as a translucent screen that reflects some of the incoming solar radiation back toward outer space. As a consequence, the insolation at the earth's surface is reduced, as are the air temperatures. The reduction can amount to a few tenths of a degree Fahrenheit and last for a year or two. The eruptions of Mount St. Helens, beginning in March 1980, discharged much less sulfur dioxide and other substances into the stratosphere than did the eruption of Mount Agung. The concentrations of atmospheric particles have been too small to cause significant global cooling or changes in weather.

CHAPTER 3
The Atmosphere and the Weather

The atmosphere can be described as an "ocean" of air that restlessly flows and tumbles, often unfelt and unseen, but sometimes tapestried with scurrying clouds and scarring the landscape with destructive winds. Chapter 2 examined the composition of the atmosphere and some of its properties. This chapter will examine such elements as temperature, pressure, and wind velocity and their interactions in fair and stormy skies.

TEMPERATURE

Air temperature normally decreases with height through the lowest 40,000 feet of the atmosphere (see Figure 2-1). This layer, called the troposphere, varies in depth from place to place and from day to day: It is most shallow over the poles and highest over low altitudes; its depth is greatest in summer and least in winter. The rate of decrease of temperature with height, called the lapse rate, is about 3.6°F per 1,000 feet in the troposphere, but varies appreciably, particularly in the lowest 1,000 feet of air.

Sometimes the temperature near the earth's surface *increases* with height. When this occurs, a *temperature inversion* is said to exist (Figure 3-1). Temperature inversions at the surface are caused when the lowest layers of air lose heat. During the evening and night, when the air is relatively dry and cloudless, energy radiates from the ground to the sky. This leads to reductions of air temperatures, starting at the surface and spreading upwards.

Long-lived inversions occur when warm air moves over a cold surface. In the United States, this happens commonly in the spring, when warm, humid air from the Gulf of Mexico sweeps north over the Great Plains and the Midwest. The ground, chilled by winter, absorbs heat from the tropical air, and temperature inversions result. Inversions in the free atmosphere— that is, away from the influence of the earth's surface—are caused when dry air sinks. When air temperature increases with height, as it does in an inversion, vertical air motions are suppressed, and the atmosphere is said to be stable.

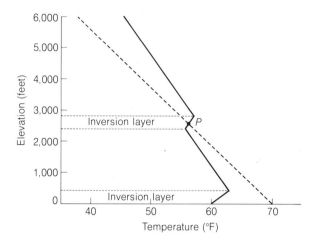

Figure 3-1 Typical variations of temperature with elevation. Notice the two inversion layers. The dashed line indicates the temperature path that would normally be taken by a volume of air at point *P* if it were to rise or sink.

A temperature inversion near the ground governs the depth of the atmosphere through which air pollutants are mixed: The stronger the inversion, the less the dispersion of pollutants and the higher their potential concentration. The horizontal spread of pollutants depends on the winds. When winds are light and temperature inversions occur at low elevations, air pollution levels can be especially high. Such temperature inversions are almost always contributing factors to major air pollution disasters, such as the one that occurred in London in 1952, as well as to the not-so-lethal pollution episodes that occur every year in many places.

PRESSURE AND WINDS

Pressure differences from place to place are the principal forces driving the winds. If the pattern of pressure is known at any level in the atmosphere, it is possible to determine the pattern of wind velocities at that level.

Pressure is the force per unit area. The weight of any substance is a force because the mass of the substance is being pulled toward the earth by gravity. *Atmospheric pressure* is the weight of a column of air divided by the area over which it rests. The weight of an air column extending from the surface to the top of the atmosphere depends mostly on the temperature of the air in the column. The higher the temperature of the air, the lighter it is and the lower its pressure at the base of the column. Water vapor in the air has a relatively small effect, but, because a molecule of water has less weight than a molecule of air, the more moist the air, the less the pressure.

At sea level, average atmospheric pressure is 14.7 pounds per square inch (psi). Atmospheric pressure is often measured by a barometer, in which a column of mercury rises or falls as the pressure changes. Barometric pressure at sea level averages 29.92 inches of mercury.

To confuse the matter further, meteorologists use still another unit of measurement, the metric millibar (mb). Average pressure at sea level is 1,013 millibars. Weather maps depict pressure patterns at sea level with isobars, that is, lines that connect places that have the same pressure (Figure 3-2). Typically, the maps show regions of high and low pressure, which continually change in size and position.

The higher you go in the atmosphere, the less air there is above you and, therefore, the lower the pressure. Air pressure always decreases with height, with the rate of decrease depending on temperature and, to a lesser extent, humidity. Average atmospheric pressure at 18,000 feet is about 7.4

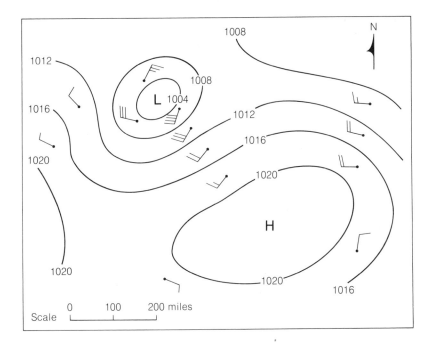

Figure 3-2   Sample pattern of surface pressure and winds. The isobars are labeled in millibars. The feathered arrows indicate wind speed and direction; the more feathers, the greater the speed. Notice that the closer the isobars, the faster the wind.

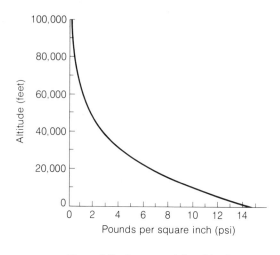

Figure 3-3 Average relationship of pressure to height in the atmosphere.

pounds per square inch (Figure 3-3). Fully half the atmospheric mass is below that altitude. At an altitude of 40 miles, average atmospheric pressure is only 0.0015 pounds per square inch. This means that more than 99.99 percent of the atmosphere is contained in a shell of air only 40 miles thick. Since the radius of the earth is about 4,000 miles, it is clear that the atmosphere is a relatively shallow layer with respect to the size of the planet.

The air moves in response to the forces acting upon it. When atmospheric pressure varies from point to point, there is a force from high to low pressure. The greater the pressure difference between two nearby points, the greater the force. If the earth were flat and did not rotate, the air would move over the surface in the direction of the pressure force. But on the nearly spherical, rotating earth with its water and land, fields and mountains, the wind is subjected to additional forces.

Air moving over a rotating sphere is subject to a force called the Coriolis force, named for the nineteenth-century French mathematician who first described it. In the Northern Hemisphere, this force acts to the right of the direction of the wind; in the Southern Hemisphere, to the left. (Since the deflection caused by this force is not a force in the precise physical sense, it is sometimes called the Coriolis effect.)

At low elevations, the surface of the earth introduces another force— friction. Friction always exists in moving systems and acts in the direction opposite to the direction of motion. When coupled with other forces, friction slows the wind and deviates it toward lower pressure. Where there is essentially no friction (in the upper atmosphere, for example), air moves along isobars—rather than across them from high to low pressure—as a result of the Coriolis force. The speed increases as the distance between isobars decreases. Because of the earth's rotation, in the Northern Hemisphere low pressure is always to the left of an observer looking downwind (see Figure 3-2). Winds blow counterclockwise around a low-pressure center and clockwise around a high-pressure center. In the Southern Hemisphere the wind directions are reversed. The air moves clockwise around a low and counterclockwise around a high.

In hilly or mountainous terrain and along coastlines, changes of temperature can lead to local winds that appear to have little relation to the overall pattern of pressure displayed on the weather maps. Along lake and ocean shores, particularly in summer, pleasant sea breezes often set in after the sun has warmed the land sufficiently more than the water. At night and in early morning, when the land is cooler than the water, a light wind sometimes blows from the land toward the lake or sea.

When skies are clear and humidities are low over orographic regions, air temperatures swing over a large range from day to night, and the wind direction does likewise. Solar radiation warming the ground and the air just above it causes breezes up valleys toward higher elevations. At night, radiation to the sky and resultant cooling lead to down-slope winds as the heavier air sinks to lower elevations.

Knowing the distribution of pressure, we can say a great deal about the weather. In general, but certainly not always, centers of low pressure, called cyclones, tend to produce cloudiness and precipitation. This occurs because, at lower elevations, air spirals into the low pressure center and rises. Centers of high pressure, called anticyclones, usually are regions of fair weather because the air swirls down toward the ground and spirals out. If weather depended only on pressure, forecasting would be easy. In fact, the weather is influenced by several other important factors, among them the atmospheric boundaries called fronts.

AIR MASSES AND FRONTS

The term *front* was coined by Scandinavian meteorologists during World War I, when there was much talk about fronts separating the Allies from the Germans. It is an appropriate term, not only because it separates contending air masses, but also because there often is a great deal of meteorological activity along a front.

The atmosphere, in a sense, is a battleground between warm and cold air masses. The former originate over tropical latitudes, where the high intensity of solar radiation heats the surface and the air. Over the oceans the air is humid as well as warm. At high latitudes, because of the relative paucity of solar radiation, the air ranges from cool to cold. It might be expected that there be a nearly smooth transition in temperature from the equator to either of the poles, but this is not the case. Cold polar air is separated from warm tropical air by a narrow zone of transition, called the polar front.

When a mass of cold air advances against one of warm air, the front separating the two is called a cold front. In cross section it resembles a blunt wedge, as the cold, heavier air pushes under the warmer, lighter air, which rises over the front (Figure 3-4). If the warm air is humid, showers and thunderstorms may occur along or ahead of the front.

Surface pressure is less along a front than ahead of or behind it. A drop in pressure accompanied by tall rain clouds indicates that a cold front may be approaching. With its passage, temperatures will drop, winds will become gusty, and pressure will rise.

When a warm front—a mass of warm air moving against one of cold air—approaches, there will be a similar sequence of pressure changes, but the temperature will rise after the front passes (Figure 3-5). A warm front resembles a sharp wedge and has a smaller slope than a cold front. The warm, overriding air rises slowly over the frontal surface, often leading to widespread clouds that produce rain or snow.

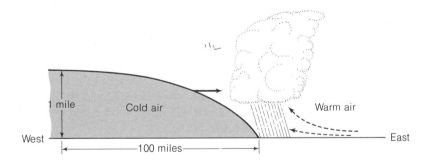

Figure 3-4   Cross section of a cold front moving west to east.

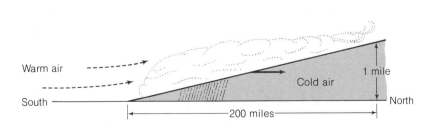

Figure 3-5   Cross section of a warm front moving south to north.

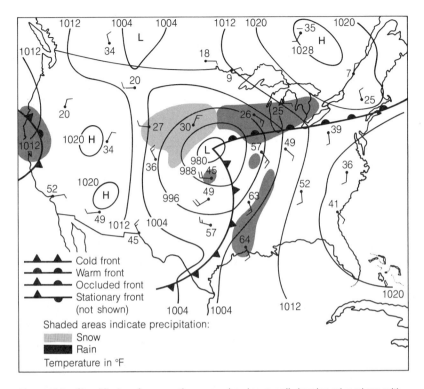

Figure 3-6 Simplified surface weather map showing a well-developed cyclone with warm and cold fronts.

When fronts moving at different speeds overtake one another, they are said to be "occluded." Occlusions commonly occur in deep cyclonic centers, where the result may be an intense rain- or snowstorm.

On weather maps, isobaric patterns show where lows and highs are located (Figure 3-6). The indicated fronts move at speeds governed by the overall wind velocities perpendicular to the fronts. In general, over the middle latitudes, weather systems tend to travel with the winds aloft, that is, from west to east. The task of a weather forecaster is to predict how the features of the map, particularly the fronts, cyclones, and anticyclones, will move and change. (See Chapter 6.)

CYCLONES

The term *cyclone* can be applied to any region of low pressure surrounded on all sides by higher pressure. Meteorologists often refer to a cyclone as a "closed low" because it is delineated on a weather map by a closed isobar surrounding the point of lowest pressure. Major winter snow- and ice storms accompanying low pressure centers associated with fronts are some-times called "frontal cyclones."

References to cyclones are often misunderstood; they usually evoke thoughts of violent weather. There is some justification for such a reaction: Over the central United States, tornadoes are commonly called cyclones; in Southeast Asia, Australia, and Mexico, the name is applied to the intense tropical storms known as hurricanes in the United States. These are not improper uses of the name, although most cyclones over the earth are centers of low pressure that do not contain threatening weather. The mid-dle latitudes of the earth experience, at regular intervals, the passage of cyclones with their associated clouds and precipitation. On weather sat-ellite photographs, cyclones sometimes have very distinctive patterns (Fig-ure 3-7). Some places see more of them than others do because there are favored regions for the formation of cyclones.

Cyclones most often develop along well-established, nearly stationary fronts. In winter, cold air from the Arctic commonly sweeps southward

Figure 3-7   Cyclone off the west coast of North America on December 31, 1978, observed by means of GOES-W satellite. (Courtesy of National Earth Satellite Service / NOAA.)

over North America behind a cold front, pushing warm air ahead of it. Usually the Rocky Mountains act as a barrier that stops the air from moving westward. As a result, the front separating the polar air over the Great Plains from warmer air becomes stationary along the eastern foothills of the Rocky Mountains.

Many cyclones develop along this front, particularly over Colorado (Figure 3-8). On a weather map, a new cyclone first appears on the front as a wavelike wiggle that coincides with an area of falling atmospheric pressure. In some cases, the wave amplitude increases and pressure continues to decrease. Clouds appear, which thicken, become widespread, and eventually yield rain or snow. As all this is going on, the cyclone usually moves more or less eastward under the influence of the major west wind currents dominating the middle latitudes.

In winter, polar air often pushes southward until the front becomes stationary in the form of a giant arc along the Gulf coast and up the eastern seaboard. Cyclones frequently develop along this front and move northward or northeastward. Many of them originate over the Gulf. Another favorite spawning ground is just off Cape Hatteras, North Carolina.

The Gulf and Hatteras storms exert a major influence on winter weather over the eastern United States. As they sweep up the coast, the warm, humid air south of the front moves up the cold frontal wedge. Near the

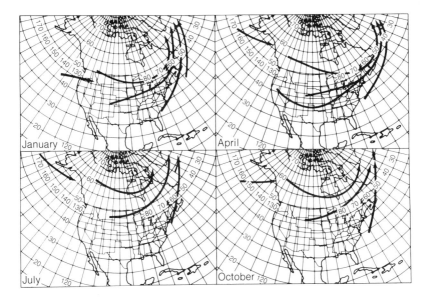

Figure 3-8 Frequent tracks of cyclones over North America during selected months. (From C. H. Reitan, *Monthly Weather Review*, December 1974.)

Figure 3-9 Heavy snowfall in Adams, New York, on February 2, 1977. (Courtesy of NOAA.)

cyclone center, the ascent of air is particularly pronounced. These storms can dump huge quantities of snow on Washington, New York, Boston, and places as far west as Cleveland (Figure 3-9). The "nor'easters" so well known in New England are cyclones of this type. They have this name because, as the cyclones progress up the Atlantic Coast, they sweep the coast with northeast winds. Occasionally the cycles are so intense that the winds reach gale force. In such circumstances, high, destructive waves of ocean water can be swept violently against the shore.

HURRICANES

As cold air from polar latitudes moves south, it gradually gains heat and moisture. The warmer the surface over which it moves, the faster it is transformed from a cold air mass to a warm one. As a result, fronts are seldom found in the tropics. Nevertheless, during the late summer and early fall, cyclones are often observed over tropical oceans.

These cyclones develop as a result of dynamical processes that cause warm, humid air over warm oceans to rise. When water vapor condenses to produce cloud droplets, heat is released in the ascending air, which leads to warming and further ascent; in a day or two, spiral bands of clouds and rain indicate the presence of a cyclone.

Over the Atlantic Ocean, this sequence usually occurs in the latitude band between 10°N and 30°N. The developing storms move generally west as they intensify and then swing north as they approach the United States. When their wind velocities exceed 73 miles per hour, tropical cyclones are called hurricanes (Figure 3-10). In extreme cases, the winds may be stronger than 150 miles per hour.

Hurricanes occur over most tropical oceans (Figure 3-11). They do not generally occur over the South Atlantic and southeastern Pacific oceans, however, for reasons unknown. Hurricanes in the western Pacific, called typhoons, significantly affect the lives of people in the Philippines, Japan, and Southeast Asia. Ciclónes, tropical cyclones that form off the south coast of Mexico, occasionally move north in their dying stages and make valuable contributions to the water supplies of southern California and Arizona.

The hurricanes that originate over the Indian Ocean can be particularly deadly, frequently devastating the low-lying coastal regions of India and neighboring countries. The most lethal hurricane in history swept over Bangladesh in November 1970, taking the lives of more than a quarter of a million people—mostly by drowning.

Figure 3-10 Hurricane Gladys, October 18, 1968, photographed from *Apollo 7*. (Courtesy of NASA.)

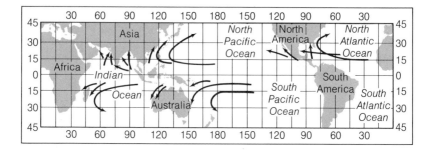

Figure 3-11 The paths of tropical cyclones. (From H. R. Byers, *General Meteorology,* 4th ed., McGraw-Hill Inc., 1974.)

Figure 3-12 Flooding of southern Louisiana on September 10, 1965, caused by Hurricane Betsy, one of the most destructive hurricanes ever to hit the United States. (Photo by R. Vetter, courtesy of American Red Cross.)

Most people associate hurricanes with strong, destructive winds: Who has not seen pictures of wind-whipped flags and palm trees? The real killer is not the wind, however, but the waves it produces. As a hurricane approaches a coast line, it causes a surge of ocean water that may be more than 10 feet high. (Over the open ocean, an intense hurricane can create waves of over 50 feet.) As this surge sweeps over the coast, it leads to massive flooding (Figure 3-12). The only salvation for people living at low elevations, such as the Florida Keys or New Orleans, is early evacuation.

When hurricanes move over land, wind speeds diminish fairly rapidly, but the flood danger still exists—not from ocean water, but from torrential rains. This is particularly true when hurricane winds blow over hilly or mountainous terrain. In June 1972, Hurricane Agnes brought about extensive inundations in Virginia, Maryland, Delaware, Pennsylvania, and New York. Damage caused by this hurricane, mostly as a result of flooding, amounted to about $3 billion.

Fortunately, weather satellites make it easy to detect and track hurricanes any place on the earth (Figure 3-13). Satellite procedures for measuring storm intensities are being improved rapidly but are not yet good enough to entirely replace other techniques. In the United States, approaching

Figure 3-13   Hurricane Allen over the Gulf of Mexico on August 8, 1980, observed by means of GOES satellite. Also note the smaller hurricane off the west coast of Mexico. (Courtesy of NOAA/EDIS.)

hurricanes are probed with specially instrumented airplanes and observed by radar.

Hurricanes are fairly large—a few hundred miles in diameter—and last for many days. No storm threatening a populated area on any continent can escape detection. In the United States, hurricane experts issue a storm "watch" when a storm is a threat to an area and a storm "warning" when it is actually approaching. But these advisories are of little value unless people in vulnerable areas know how to protect themselves. Residents of areas bordering the Gulf of Mexico and the southern Atlantic Coast, particularly, should contact the Federal Emergency Management Agency experts in their areas for advice.* During the hurricane season—from July to October—it is wise to have a battery-operated radio or television set in the event of a major storm.

THUNDERSTORMS AND TORNADOES

In spite of the enormous damage hurricanes can cause, the rain they bring is vital to life in the regions that experience them. Equally as important and dangerous are the smaller, much shorter lived phenomena—thunderstorms and tornadoes.

Thunderstorms, because they are most frequent in spring and summer, are critically important and welcome visitors over the grain belts of the world, where they are the principal source of water during the growing season. Over the United States, thunderstorms occur most often in Florida and along the coast of the Gulf of Mexico (Figure 3-14).

The most severe long-lasting storms, the ones that produce hail and tornadoes, are commonly associated with cold fronts. On the other hand, many thunderstorms occur far away from fronts. They form when the air is warm and humid and the atmosphere is unstable, a condition that exists when the temperature decreases markedly with height.

A thunderstorm begins as a rising column of air that produces a white, cauliflowerlike cloud. Within the growing cloud are turbulent rising columns of air, called updrafts, that in a severe storm can exceed speeds of 60 miles per hour. Such a storm can extend to a height of over 60,000 feet. When it encounters the stable stratosphere, the cloud spreads out, mostly downwind, and takes on the form of a giant anvil (Figure 3-15). Most often

---

*The Federal Emergency Management Agency, often called FEMA, is responsible for developing procedures to protect the public from natural or man-made catastrophes. Experts in FEMA work with meteorologists at the National Weather Service and officials of the state and local governments.

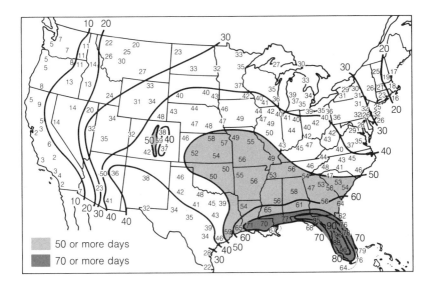

Figure 3-14 Mean number of days with thunderstorms per year, based on data for 1951–1975. (From A. Court and J. F. Griffiths, *Thunderstorms*, Vol. 2, E. Kessler, ed., U.S. Government Printing Office, 1982.)

Figure 3-15 Thunderstorm with anvil, photographed near Denver on August 4, 1976. (Photo by Charles Semmer, courtesy of NCAR/NSF.)

the growth of a thunderstorm is impeded by a stable layer—sometimes a temperature inversion—that serves as a lid over the cloud top.

As a thunderstorm matures, a downdraft develops adjacent to the updraft core. Both drafts are composed of churning high-speed air resembling a tumbling stream of rushing water. This pattern of air motion accounts for the turbulence experienced by an airplane flying through a thunderstorm. The drafts may carry an airplane up or down while eddies in air velocity buffet it and, in extreme cases, cause structural damage.

Most thunderstorms pass through their lifetimes in less than an hour, yielding a few lightning strokes and rain. Provided no one is struck by lightning, these storms do a great deal more good than harm. The rain is usually very beneficial, particularly to farms. The cool air that precedes an arriving thunderstorm on a hot summer day is the result of air from high altitudes being cooled by the evaporation of water drops; the air descends to the ground and spreads out, mostly in the direction of the storm motion.

Some thunderstorms, because of their large sizes and long durations, are called "supercell" thunderstorms. They can last for many hours and have strong, persistent updrafts and downdrafts. They commonly occur as parts of a squall line, a line of thunderstorms, often oriented northeast–southwest, that sweeps across the Great Plains ahead of an advancing cold front.

Supercell storms can produce violent weather. They are the sources of tornadoes and hail. As these storms move over the flatlands of Kansas, Nebraska, Iowa, Illinois, and surrounding states, they sometimes lay down swaths of hail that devastate wheat, corn, and soybeans (Figure 3-16). In an average year, hail damage to agriculture in the United States amounts to more than $700 million.

Hailstorms also cause widespread damage in many other parts of the world: the fruit orchards of northern Italy, the grapevines of the Caucasus region of the Soviet Union, the tea plantations in Kenya, the farmlands of South Africa and Argentina. In India, 246 people were killed during a severe hailstorm near New Delhi in April 1888.

Surprisingly, lightning—the phenomenon that essentially identifies a thunderstorm—kills more people than any other circumstance of weather, with the exception of flash floods. Because of the interaction of water and ice particles and of the vertical motions in thunderclouds, electric charges accumulate on cloud droplets. The charges in the upper parts of the cloud usually are mostly positive, while those in the lower parts are mostly negative. When the quantities of charges become large enough, a giant electrical spark—lightning—flashes from one cloud region to another or from cloud to ground. On the average, in the United States, lightning accounts for about 200 deaths each year, while hurricanes and tornadoes combined cause about 190. During a thunderstorm, lightning poses a serious hazard

Figure 3-16 Hail damage to a corn crop. (Courtesy of NCAR/NSF.)

to anyone in open spaces. A wise person gets off the golf course or out of a boat and gets inside a building or an automobile. It is especially dangerous under an isolated tree. A person struck by lightning is usually knocked unconscious and stops breathing; the person will die unless breathing is begun within minutes. The quick use of artificial respiration procedures sometimes can save the victim's life.

Figure 3-17 Tornado near Union City, Oklahoma, May 24, 1973. (Photo by Joseph Demmer. Courtesy of NSSL/NOAA.)

Thunderstorms also are the source of tornadoes (Figure 3-17). There still is considerable debate among the experts about how tornadoes form, but it has to do with the effects of the vertical air motions in concentrating, already existing rotational air motions. Most tornadoes are cyclonic—blowing counterclockwise in the Northern Hemisphere—but a funnel will occasionally be anticyclonic. Typically, tornadoes are less than a quarter of a mile in diameter and last for only a few minutes, but some are larger and may last for a few hours or more. These tend to be the most violent, destructive, and deadly.

The danger from tornadoes comes from the strong winds (sometimes exceeding 200 miles per hour) and the low pressure in the center of the vortex. In combination, these factors lead to the virtual explosions of buildings because of pressure differences inside and outside the buildings. The strong winds pick up and carry debris, presenting a major hazard to living creatures not under cover.

Although the statistics on tornado fatalities are not as high as might be expected, the enormous destructive power of a tornado is frightening. A tornado can destroy a neighborhood in minutes, decimating houses and leaving only the foundations. Tornadoes can also do totally unpredictable things: They can pick people up, carry them through the air, and deposit them unhurt; they can strip chickens of their feathers or pick up railroad cars and move houses. Occasionally a tornado will totally destroy a building and leave one unscratched only a few feet away.

The following excerpt from the records of the National Weather Service illustrates the often bizarre results of a tornado:

> Some unusual features were: a government bond found 60 miles southeast of Eldorado address, eight $100 bills found intact in envelope far from owner's home in Eldorado, boy found with dozen splintered sticks protruding from his chest, woman sucked through window and blown 60 feet from house, and beside her was found a broken record entitled 'Stormy Weather,' automobile carried more than a block and jammed through roof between a bed and a dresser . . .

Tornadoes occur in many countries, but nowhere are they as frequent and as violent as in the United States, where more than 700 tornadoes are reported annually. Tornado-producing thunderstorms occur most often over the Great Plains and the Midwest in spring and early summer (Figure 3-18). Florida and nearby states also have a high frequency of tornadoes, many of which may be imbedded in a single hurricane.

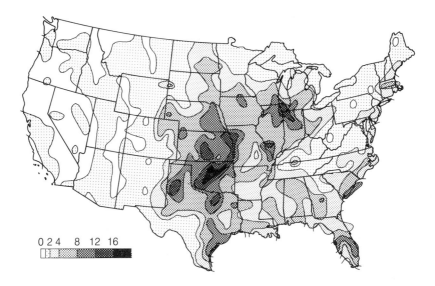

0 2 4 8 12 16

Figure 3-18 Average number of tornadoes per year per 10,000 square miles, based on state averages for 1955–1967. The distribution of major hailstorm frequency is similar to that of tornado frequency. (Prepared by M. L. Swift from data by M. E. Pautz. From A. Court, "The Climate of the Conterminous United States," *Climates of North America*, Vol. 11, R. A. Bryson and F. K. Hare, eds., Elsevier, Amsterdam, 1973.)

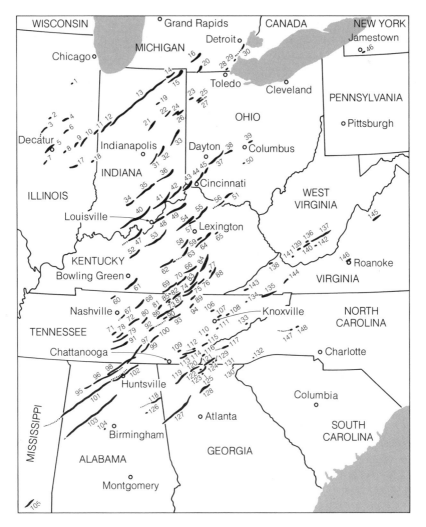

Figure 3-19 Tornado tracks during 24-hour period beginning noon Central Standard Time, April 3, 1974. (Diagram based on analyses made by T. T. Fujita, from R. F. Abbey, Jr., and T. T. Fujita, *Thunderstorms: A Social, Scientific and Technical Documentary,* Vol. 1, U.S. Government Printing Office, 1982.)

Tornadoes tend to form in families; when one develops, more are likely. The most extensive outbreak of tornadoes ever recorded in the United States took place in April 1974, when 148 tornadoes were observed over the eastern half of the country in two days (Figure 3-19). The costs were extreme: 315 dead; 6,142 injured; and $600 million in damage.

When National Weather Service forecasters expect tornadoes to occur over the next few hours, they issue a tornado watch. When a funnel has been spotted or radar observations indicate that one is present, a tornado warning is issued. There is little that can be done to protect property, but proper planning can reduce the risks of injury and deaths. The National Weather Service has issued the following safety rules:

If outdoors with no shelter available, lie flat in a nearby ditch. Shield your head with your arms. In a car or truck, do not try to drive away from the funnel. Leave your vehicle for a ditch.

Stay away from windows, doors, and outside walls in homes. Go to the basement or an interior part on the lowest level.

Get under something sturdy. Protect your head.

Move to designated shelter areas in schools, hospitals, shopping centers, and other public places. Interior hallways on lowest floors are best.

Leave mobile homes for more substantial shelter.*

Bulletin of American Meteorological Society, Vol. 62, April 1981.

CHAPTER 4
Water and the Atmosphere

In terms of water, Earth is unique among the planets in our solar system. Most of the earth's water is contained in the oceans, which cover about 70 percent of its surface. In the atmosphere, the volume of water, preponderantly in the form of vapor, is about 3,400,000 billion gallons. But this represents only 0.001 percent of the aqueous substance on the earth (Table 4-1). Another 0.627 percent of terrestrial water is found in lakes and streams or underground. These statistics show that although there is an enormous supply of water on the earth, only a small fraction is readily available for agricultural, industrial, and municipal use. Someday it will become necessary to tap the vast supplies of salt water, but at present, the cost of converting salt water to fresh water makes it too expensive in comparison to the prices charged for naturally fresh water.

Although terrestrial water in the atmosphere is but a small percentage of the total, it profoundly influences the lives of everyone. The water vapor in the air is converted to rain and snow that waters farm lands, fills reservoirs, and replenishes overpumped aquifers—underground layers of permeable rock, sand, or gravel. Precipitation feeds the rivers and streams that supply water for cities and towns, for irrigation, and for powering hydroelectric plants. The raindrops and ice particles that constitute precipitation are the end products of a series of processes that begin with the formation of clouds.

Table 4-1 Water Content of the Earth

Location	Water in billions of gallons	Percent of total
Oceans	349,000,000,000	97.220
Icecaps and glaciers	7,700,000,000	2.145
Rivers, lakes, and soil	2,250,000,000	0.627
Salty lakes and inland seas	27,000,000	0.008
Atmosphere	3,400,000	0.001
TOTAL	358,980,400,000	

CLOUDS

A cloud is a visible assemblage of small water droplets or ice crystals. The droplets, about 3,000 per cubic inch of cloud, typically have diameters ranging from microscopic size to 0.002 inch. Droplets form as a result of condensation of water vapor on tiny atmospheric particles, called condensation nuclei, which are mostly sulfate aerosols formed in the atmosphere or grains of sea salt remaining after the evaporation of ocean spray. Condensation begins when the relative humidity of the air approaches saturation. If the concentration of water vapor in the air remains constant, relative humidity increases as air temperature decreases. For this reason, most clouds occur as a result of cooling.

On clear nights when the air near the ground is fairly humid, the loss of heat by outward radiation can increase the relative humidity enough to cause the condensation known as dew to form on cool objects, such as leaves. The decrease in air temperature in the lowest layers of the atmosphere is sometimes sufficient for condensation to take place on nuclei in the air. In such a circumstance, a cloud is created in the form of fog. These radiation fogs form first in low-lying places—valleys and dips in the road—because the coldest, heaviest air flows into them. Fogs sometimes yield a fine drizzle, but, except in places where the droplets are intercepted by trees, the amount of precipitation is very small.

Most clouds, particularly those that yield appreciable rain and snow, come into being because of the ascent of air. When a volume of air rises, it moves into regions of lower and lower atmospheric pressure (see Figure 3-3), and the air volume expands. Since energy is expended in the expansion, this process leads to a reduction in temperature. The rate of decrease of temperature with height, called the dry adiabatic lapse rate, is nearly constant—about 5.4°F per 1,000 feet (Figure 4-1).

As the temperature of the ascending air decreases, the relative humidity increases. The more humid the air at the outset, the less the amount of lifting needed to begin condensation and cloud formation. In other words, the higher the humidity at the ground, the lower the cloud base. For this reason, summer cloud bases in humid Florida are about 2,000 feet above sea level, while in Arizona, where the air is drier, they are about five times higher.

Once cloud formation begins, a rising volume of air gains heat from the condensation process itself. As explained in Chapter 2, evaporation requires heat and leads to cooling. The reverse process, condensation, releases heat and leads to warming. In a rising volume of cloud air, the heat is sufficient to reduce the lapse rate from 5.4°F per 1,000 feet to a lower rate, varying with the air temperature but averaging 3.3°F per 1,000 feet in the lower atmosphere. (See Figure 4-1.)

As cloud air rises, the minute droplets rapidly assume the temperatures of the surrounding air. Often a growing cloud extends above the level

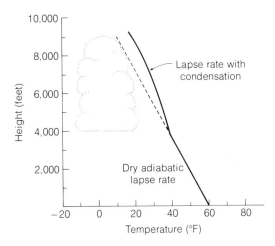

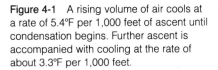

Figure 4-1   A rising volume of air cools at a rate of 5.4°F per 1,000 feet of ascent until condensation begins. Further ascent is accompanied with cooling at the rate of about 3.3°F per 1,000 feet.

where the temperature is 32°F, the normal freezing level. Sometimes the water droplets in such a cloud freeze, and the cloud consists of tiny ice crystals. At other times, the water droplets do not freeze even when temperatures are very low. Such droplets are said to be supercooled. When the water is extremely clean and devoid of substances that can serve as nuclei around which ice can grow, water can be supercooled to as low as −40°F. But in the atmosphere, clouds are seldom supercooled to temperatures below about 0°F. The air usually contains large numbers of nuclei that cause ice crystals to form at temperatures between about 5°F and 15°F. Most ice nuclei are composed of particular types of soil particles, often kaolinite and montmorillonite.

The great variation in cloud types is obvious to even the casual observer. Clouds vary in shape, height, thickness, texture, color, and optical effects. The shape and height of a cloud depend, to a large extent, on the processes that bring it into being, particularly the pattern of vertical air motions.

The World Meteorological Organization has adopted, with relatively few changes, a system of cloud classification founded by Luke Howard, an Englishman whose 1804 essay named and defined four general cloud types: stratus, cumulus, cirrus, and nimbus. The German poet Goethe was so impressed that he composed a poem, entitled "To the Honoured Memory of Howard," with four stanzas given the cloud names that Howard introduced. Meteorologists generally do not consider nimbus a cloud type, but use the word as a prefix or suffix to designate rain- or snow-producing clouds.

Figure 4-2 Stratus cloud. (Courtesy of NOAA.)

Figure 4-3 A cirrostratus, composed of ice crystals, sometimes produces a halo. (Photo by Grant W. Goode, courtesy of NOAA.)

Figure 4-4   An altostratus, composed of water droplets, often produces a corona around the sun. (Courtesy of NOAA.)

When conditions are suitable for the formation of fog but winds are brisk, a layer of cloud droplets can form a few hundred feet above the ground. The resulting uniform, gray deck is a stratus cloud (Figure 4-2). Occasionally, rain falling into cold air under a warm front can moisten the air enough to cause the formation of ragged stratus clouds. Air slowing gliding up a warm front leads to widespread layer clouds at various altitudes. The same condition is sometimes found in cyclones, as the air rises slowly—less than a foot per second—over regions a few hundred miles across. The resulting formation of high clouds composed of ice crystals is called a cirrostratus (Figure 4-3). A formation of nonprecipitating clouds in uniform layers at medium altitudes is called an altostratus (Figure 4-4) Stratified rain and snow clouds are called nimbostratus.

Cirrus clouds occur at high elevations, where temperatures are so cold that the clouds are composed mostly of ice crystals. They appear as white, featherlike streaks or bands (Figure 4-5). Some cirrus take the form of bright patches with silky trails. This occurs when wave motions at high elevations cause updrafts strong enough to cause the start of condensation and ice crystal formation. When the crystals collide and stick, they become snowflakes and fall out of the original cloud tuft. The flakes follow a

Figure 4-5   Cirrus clouds. (Courtesy of NOAA.)

curving trajectory that depends on their fall speeds and the wind. As the particles fall, they evaporate and ultimately disappear.

Cumulus clouds resemble domes or towers with appreciable vertical extent. Their upper parts, which often resemble cauliflowers, are a brilliant white in sunlight. As cumuli grow, they are called cumulus congestus (Figure 4-6) and, ultimately, cumulonimbus, which commonly produce thunderstorms (Figure 4-7).

Cumulus clouds are often called convective clouds because they are the result of convection, a process of heat transfer in which warm, light air rises while cool, heavy air sinks. When the temperature is particularly warm at low altitudes compared with the temperature aloft—specifically, when the rate of decrease of air temperature is greater than the dry adiabatic lapse rate—the atmosphere is unstable and conducive to convection. This means that if a volume of air is given an upward impulse, perhaps because of the lifting effects of a cold front, the air continues moving up. The greater the rate of decrease of temperature with height in relation to the adiabatic lapse rate, the greater the updraft velocity. Updrafts in thunderstorms often have speeds as high as 20 miles per hour and, in rare cases, over 60 miles per hour. As the storm develops, downdrafts appear, sometimes exceeding 50 miles per hour in the mature stage of a thunderstorm.

A fascinating personal account of the internal properties of an active thunderstorm was given by Lieutenant Colonel William A. Rankin, who on July 26, 1959, bailed out from a crippled F8U Crusader into a thunderstorm at 47,000 feet. A long, frightening free fall took him to about

Figure 4-6   Cumulus congestus clouds over San Xavier Mission, Tucson, Arizona. (Photo by John P. Schaefer.)

Figure 4-7   Cumulonimbus producing rainstorm. (Courtesy of NOAA.)

Figure 4-8 Mountain wave clouds (altocumulus) (Courtesy of NCAR/NSF.)

10,000 feet, where his parachute opened. In normal circumstances he should have hit the ground about 10 minutes later. Instead, he was caught up in a series of updrafts and downdrafts and, for *40 minutes*, he was pelted by raindrops and hailstones and shaken by nearby lightning and thunder.*

Over mountainous terrain, relatively shallow clouds can contain strong updrafts. They occur when strong winds blow over a ridge and take on a wavy pattern downwind of the ridge. If the air is sufficiently humid, clouds form in the rising portions of the waves. These clouds can take on various shapes, occasionally resembling large stacks of pancakes or beautiful three-dimensional forms (Figure 4-8). These are altocumulus clouds, a name indicating that they are located at medium altitudes and have some cumuliform characteristics. Cumuliform clouds arranged in layers at low altitudes are called stratocumulus (Figure 4-9).

There are many other types and configurations of clouds in addition to the ones described here. But these are the clouds that you will most likely see when you look at the sky.

RAIN AND SNOW

For the condensed water in clouds to be of use in growing vegetation or in meeting the needs of municipalities or industry, the water must precipitate out of the atmosphere—fall to the surface. This happens when the water drops or ice particles are large enough to survive the trip without

---

*William A. Rankin, *The Man Who Rode the Thunder*, Prentice-Hall, 1960.

Figure 4-9   Stratocumulus clouds. (Courtesy of NOAA.)

evaporating completely. As you would expect, the higher the cloud base
and the lower the relative humidity of the air, the greater a water drop
must be to survive the trip to the ground. In general, a water drop with a
diameter of less than 0.01 inch is not likely to reach the surface. Raindrops
typically have diameters of about 0.05 inch. They are seldom larger than
0.2 inch, as they tend to break up beyond that limit. The diameter of a
raindrop is about one-sixth the diameter of the splash mark it makes on a
cement sidewalk.

Condensation alone cannot account for rain and snow. That process is
responsible for the formation of cloud elements, but, except in unusual
circumstances, it will not produce droplets large enough to precipitate. A
raindrop 0.1 inch in diameter contains a million times more water than a
cloud droplet 0.001 inch in diameter. To account for such aggregation,
processes in addition to condensation must come into play. Two such
processes help explain the growth of raindrops.

In many clouds, particularly over the warmer regions of the earth, rain
is produced by the collision and coalescence of cloud droplets. Condensation produces cloud droplets with diameters ranging from about 0.0002
inch to perhaps 0.002 inch. The larger ones fall faster than the smaller

ones and intercept them. As this process goes on, the larger droplets increase to the size of raindrops.

The other process that leads to rain and frozen precipitation requires the coexistence of water and ice particles in a supercooled cloud. Because of differences in the physical properties of water and ice, the water droplets evaporate while the ice crystals grow. This occurs most rapidly at temperatures close to 10°F, but it works throughout the range of supercooling occurring in the atmosphere. The type of ice crystals formed—needles, plates, or dendrites (Figure 4-10)—depends mostly on the temperature at

Figure 4-10 Forms of ice crystals. Top to bottom: needles, plates, two types of dendrites. (From W. A. Bentley and W. J. Humphreys, *Snow Crystals*, Dover Publications Inc., 1962.)

which the crystals grow. As they enlarge, they fall through the cloud and collide with supercooled water droplets, which freeze to them, and with other crystals, which stick to them. The result is precipitation in the form of snowflakes.

If the air below the clouds is at subfreezing temperatures, the snow can reach the ground. But when snowflakes fall into a layer of warm air, they melt and become raindrops. In mountainous areas, it is common for rain to fall in the valleys and snow to cover the higher elevations (Figure 4-11).

One of the most dangerous forms of precipitation is freezing rain. It usually occurs under a warm front during the cold seasons of the year. The sequence of events leading to freezing rain begins when snowflakes grow in subfreezing stratiform clouds above the warm front. When the air just over the front is warm enough, the snowflakes melt. The resulting raindrops then fall through the front into the cold air below. If temperatures are only slightly below 32°F, the raindrops can reach the ground without freezing. However, upon striking cold surfaces, such as power lines, tree branches, and pavement, the water freezes, leaving a slick, treacherous coating of ice known as glaze (Figure 4-12).

Figure 4-11   In mountainous areas, snow may fall at high elevations while rain occurs in the valleys. Note the multilayered lens-shaped altocumulus in the upper left-hand corner. (Courtesy of Glenn Gordon, University of Wyoming.)

56

Figure 4-12   Freezing rain on telephone lines. (Courtesy of NOAA.)

If the cold air under the front is very cold, the falling raindrops may freeze and become ice pellets, generally less than 0.2 inch in diameter, called sleet. The word is commonly employed in Britain and some parts of the United States to designate a mixture of rain and snow.

Frozen precipitation sometimes takes the form of white, opaque particles smaller than 0.2 inch in diameter. These are called snow pellets; unlike their icy counterparts, they are soft and easily crushed.

Ice particles with diameters greater than 0.2 inch are considered hailstones. In extreme cases they can be bigger than oranges. The largest hailstone on record in the United States fell at Coffeyville, Kansas, on September 3, 1970. It had a circumference of 17.3 inches and weighed 1.67 pounds (Figure 4-13).

The water brought to the ground by hail is welcomed when it falls on grazing land or in a watershed without cultivated agriculture. On the other hand, as noted in Chapter 3, the damage caused by hailstones to crops is high. Most farmers and fruit growers prefer to receive their atmospheric water in liquid form.

Figure 4-13 The largest hailstone ever recorded in the United States. (Courtesy of NCAR/NSF.)

FLOODS

We cannot live without rain, but sometimes it comes in such great quantities that we cannot live with it, either. When too much rain falls in too short a time, the result is a flood (Figure 4-14). In the United States, estimated flood losses average about $2 billion a year and are expected to increase as more homes and other structures are built in flood-prone areas. The National Water Resources Council has predicted that annual flood damages will average $3.5 billion by the year 2000 unless flood plain management is improved.

Floods are a normal component of the human experience—they have always been with us and, in all likelihood, always will be. In the future, we probably will learn how to exert some effective controls over how much rain and snow falls, but not to the extent necessary to prevent the occurrence of floods. Therefore, we have to learn to live with them, minimizing the losses of life and property and maximizing the use of the water for socially advantageous purposes.

58

Figure 4-14 Flooding near Wilkes-Barre, Pennsylvania, caused by Hurricane Agnes, June 1972. (Courtesy of the U.S. Coast Guard.)

Floods can be divided into two classes: One results from more or less continuous rainfall over a large region for an extended period of time. This can lead to major floods that cover millions of acres and that may go on for weeks. A second class is composed of "flash floods," which result from relatively short periods of very heavy rains. They develop rapidly and usually last only a few hours or less. But, because of their sudden onset and the fact that huge walls of water sometimes come rushing down narrow valleys or canyons, flash floods are very dangerous.

The most widespread flooding in the United States generally occurs in the spring over the vast river basin in the Midwest. This includes the area near the Mississippi River and its northern tributaries, the Ohio and Missouri rivers. The general sequence of events leading to major floods in this region has been repeated time and again: During a cold, wet winter, a blanket of snow is deposited over the Midwest and Great Plains states. If temperatures are sufficiently cold, the ground freezes and snow accumulates, with relatively little melting. In the spring, a cyclonic storm that includes a warm, humid mass of tropical air moving north yields heavy rains over an area hundreds of miles wide. The rain added to the melting snow results in large quantities of water rushing towards lower elevations. When the ground is frozen, little water is absorbed by the soil.

Even when there is no snow on the ground, cyclonic storms that move slowly or stagnate for several days can cause floods in any location. Continuous precipitation over a day or two nearly saturates the soil. Once this happens, the water begins to accumulate on the land and flow downhill.

When the volume of water exceeds the carrying capacity of the streams and channels, the water overflows the bank and covers cities and farms. In extreme circumstances, it can be many weeks before the water level drops enough to allow people to return to their homes and places of employment.

The floods caused by large cyclonic storms tend to develop slowly. People can leave hazardous areas before the water rises to life-threatening levels—but if the water overruns banks and dikes, little can be done to protect property.

On the other hand, flash floods set in so rapidly that in many cases people are caught in the flood waters. Flash floods kill more people than all other weather-related disasters. The average death toll in the United States now runs about 200 per year, more than twice as great as in the 1960s. Flash floods are caused by violent weather events such as thunderstorms and hurricanes. There have been some spectacular examples in recent years. In July 1976, a large thunderstorm system deluged the western third of the Big Thompson Canyon in Colorado with 12 inches of rain in less than 6 hours. The resulting flood rushing down the canyon took at least 139 lives.

Hurricane Agnes, mentioned earlier, dropped torrential rains on five eastern seaboard states. Harrisburg, Pennsylvania, measured more than 13 inches of rain over 24 hours ending on June 22, 1972. The five-state area flooded by the hurricane had 120 storm-related fatalities.

To minimize the loss of life and economic hardship requires comprehensive programs of watershed and flood plain management. In the past, the emphasis has been on flood control and protection—the construction of dams and dikes and similar measures. In recent years, increasing attention has been given to a variety of procedures for improving flood warnings and public response as well as land management. Special instruments have been developed for the early detection of heavy rainfall over areas having high risks of floods. Flood-hazard studies have led to zoning changes that discourage building in areas where the risks of floods are high. Federally supported flood insurance programs have been designed to assist people who suffer flood losses. Clearly, to minimize the risks of floods and their costs in life and property, systematic assessments of relevant factors and the development of comprehensive management procedures are essential.

DROUGHTS

The term *drought* is defined in the dictionary as "prolonged dry weather." You may wonder, how prolonged and how dry? It just is not possible to give an all-inclusive answer; it is easier to identify a drought by its consequences. If corn is dying in the fields for lack of water, a drought is occurring. If cattle on an open range suffer because of empty water holes, the same can be said. When a large city has to reduce lawn sprinkling and use of air conditioners, a drought has hit the area.

In effect, when living organisms are suffering because of a deficiency of rainfall, a drought is present. Thus, the criterion for the existence of a drought is more biological than meteorological.

Meteorologists have sought to derive a definition based on rainfall, but, because of the complicated and variable relationship of weather, soil moisture, plants, and animals, none has been entirely satisfactory. It is obvious, however, that the less the actual rainfall compared with the long-term average rainfall, the greater the likelihood of a drought.

Every year, some parts of the United States suffer droughts, causing average losses of wheat and corn alone exceeding 100 million and 500 million bushels per year, respectively. During the severe, widespread droughts of 1934–1937 and 1952–1956, losses were much greater than the average annual amounts.

In some regions, such as the northeastern United States, a year of 20 inches of rain would be a year of drought (Figure 4-15). On the other hand,

Figure 4-15   The effects of a drought. (From The National Archives; courtesy N. J. Rosenberg.)

the same quantity of rainfall in southern Arizona would represent a year of water abundance. The damage suffered by plants during a drought depends not only on rainfall, but also on the species of the plant and the properties of the soil. Therefore, even in a single region, a prolonged dry spell may harm some plant communities and not others.

The prolonged dry spell in the northeastern United States during the early and middle 1960s made that part of the country more conscious than ever of the importance of rain and snow. But in many places, fresh water is thought of as being inexhaustible and of relatively little value. In most parts of the United States there are few restrictions on water for personal use. A shower a day is regarded as an inalienable right. Watering the lawn, washing the car, filling the swimming pool, not fixing the leaky faucet— these also appear to be every person's privileges. As long as the number of uses and users is relatively small and the atmosphere feeds the reservoirs in normal amounts, the availability of cheap water is taken for granted.

When nature cuts the water supply by a quarter or a half and consumption goes on at a luxurious rate, however, enormous problems arise. River flows diminish, and reservoirs dry up. Along the coasts, the quantity of fresh water going from rivers into oceans decreases, and salt water begins to advance, first toward the rivers, then up their channels. This can continue until the intake pipes for fresh water begin drawing brine, as almost happened in Philadelphia in the summer of 1965, when ocean water began invading the Delaware River.

By the summer of 1967, the rainfall in the eastern United States had returned to nearly normal. New York City reservoirs were near 100 percent of capacity, up from 40 percent in 1965. As a consequence, concerns for long-range planning for water supplies gradually faded. Unfortunately, droughts do come back, and in 1981 New Yorkers were again facing water shortages.

America does not have a monopoly on droughts. They happen all over the world, sometimes in many places at the same time. When they occur in the major grain growing regions, they make themselves known in the international grain markets. To this extent droughts, particularly the widespread, persistent ones, are global problems. By means of satellite observations and more standard, ground-based measurements, droughts around the world are monitored by scientists at the Center for Environmental Assessment Services of the National Oceanic and Atmospheric Administration in Washington, D.C. The data are used by agricultural specialists to estimate food production in the United States and other countries and by others concerned with social and political problems that arise from droughts.

CHAPTER 5
Climate and the General Circulation

In the *Glossary of Meteorology* (American Meteorological Society, Boston, 1959), C. S. Durst describes the climate as "the synthesis of the weather." More specifically, it can be defined as the collected statistics of weather conditions of a specific area for a specified period of time. In more general terms, the climate of an area is indicated by long-term averages of various weather elements and variations above and below those averages.

These definitions leave certain points unresolved. For example, over how long should the averages be taken? The answer is somewhat arbitrary, depending on what one intends to do with the results. Some scientists, concerned with planetary climatic variations over the last century, have used 10-year averages of global temperature. Paleoclimatologists, studying changes in climate over *millions* of years, rely on geological and fossil data and might take averages over millennia. It is critically important to know the time periods and geographical areas involved. Sometimes these are implicit and obvious, but at other times they must be stated explicitly.

In general, the averaging period should be long enough to smooth out the inevitable short-period fluctuations of relatively minor importance. Recognizing that the weather can change drastically from year to year and by significant amounts from one decade to the next, climatologists concluded that several decades of data would be needed to give statistics that varied slowly. The International Meteorological Conference in Warsaw in 1933 agreed upon a 30-year averaging period. Accepted practice is to compute, every 10 years, averages of the weather elements for the preceding 3 decades and to designate them "normal" values of the weather elements.

Most of the major cities of the world have each had one or more weather stations for many decades—in some cases for centuries. Statistical analyses have yielded volumes of climatic data and data summaries. (See Appendix I.) Climatologists have used such information to classify the climates of the earth, region by region, in categories corresponding to the wetness and temperatures of an area. The greater the precipitation in relation to the amount of water that can be lost by evaporation and transpiration, the greater the wetness. In places devoid of measurements of temperatures and precipitation, natural vegetation types have been used as climatic indicators.

Over recent decades, interest in the overall global climate has been increasing. Is it warming or cooling, and how can the changes be explained? This is not a new problem by any means. For a very long time, philosophers and scientists have wondered about the causes of the ice ages and the advance and retreat of glaciers and sea ice. Climatic changes over geological times will be discussed later in this chapter. We will first consider how the climate varies over periods of decades and centuries, and the factors governing these variations.

THE GENERAL CIRCULATION

Since the climate is largely an integral function of the weather, it is necessary to examine the general factors governing the weather. A meteorologist might say that the climate depends on the general circulation of the atmosphere—that is, the average global patterns of pressure, wind, and related weather.

The general circulation of the atmosphere depends on such factors as its composition, the earth's rotation, the arrangement of continents and oceans, and the quantity and distribution of incoming solar radiation. The earth rotates about its axis once every 24 hours; its orbit around the sun takes about 365 days. Because of the tilt of the earth's axis with respect to the plane of its orbit, solar energy north of the equator is most intense in June. Six months later, the sun is south of the equator, and maximum radiation falls on the Southern Hemisphere. This shift of the earth relative to the sun accounts for the seasons.

Over a year, the earth's equatorial regions intercept more solar energy than do more poleward latitudes. If there were no air or ocean currents, the lower latitudes would be appreciably warmer than they are now, while polar regions would be appreciably colder. The wind and ocean currents of the earth serve to transfer heat poleward and maintain the balance that exists today.

On the average, wind patterns at lower latitudes resemble a giant convection cell, wherein warm air rises over the equatorial zone and moves poleward in the upper troposphere, while near the surface the air moves equatorward. The air aloft sinks towards the ground in large anticyclones centered at latitudes of about 30°.

In the centers of anticyclones, skies tend to be clear and winds light. Sailing ships caught in the center of one of the large persistent highs, such as the one normally centered near Bermuda in July, could be stalled for long periods. It is said that when feed and water ran low, horses that were to be used at the destination sometimes were dropped overboard—hence the name "horse latitudes."

Through the middle latitudes—from about 30° to 60°—there is a broad region where westerly winds prevail throughout the troposphere.* A distinctive feature of the west-wind belt is a narrow current of strong winds often found at altitudes of 30,000 feet to 40,000 feet. Because the wind speeds are so high—sometimes exceeding 200 miles per hour—and concentrated, this current is called the jet stream. It occurs over the polar front, the boundary between cold polar air and warm tropical air. The jet stream plays an important role in the formation and life history of cyclones and hence is an important element in explaining the weather and climate of the earth.

The jet is stronger and further away from the poles in the winter than in the summer. Typically it meanders south and north as it circles nearly the entire earth. The northern limit of the westerly wind belt is delineated by two deep centers of low pressure, one near Iceland and the other in the Gulf of Alaska. Closer to the poles, the wind is mostly easterly near the ground. Air sinks over the poles and rises along latitude belts at about 60°.

This simplified description of the wind pattern over the earth is a general overview. Figure 5-1 shows observed averages of surface pressures and winds over the earth in January and July. These maps represent the general circulation of the lower atmosphere. The existence of oceans and land affect the pressure and winds. In winter, air temperatures are lower and surface pressures are higher over the land than over the water, while the reverse is true in summer. As a result of the pressure patterns, air tends to blow from land to water in winter and from water to land in summer. These seasonal winds are known as monsoons.

Sinking motions over the latitude belts between about 20° and 40° occur in the series of semipermanent high-pressure centers in the Northern and Southern hemispheres. Between these bands of high pressure, the winds blow toward the equator with an easterly component. These are the trade winds that played such an important role in the days of sailing vessels. The heavy line on each of the maps of Figure 5-1 indicates the boundary between the northeast trade winds and the southeast trade winds.

The features of the general circulation over a region greatly affect the region's climate. When high pressure and subsiding air prevail, cloud formation is inhibited and precipitation is light (Figure 5-2). For this reason, the arid and semiarid regions—the deserts of the world—are generally found where semipermanent highs occur. Heavy precipitation is found in

---

*Wind direction is indicated by the direction from which it is blowing; for example, a *west* or *westerly* wind blows from the west.

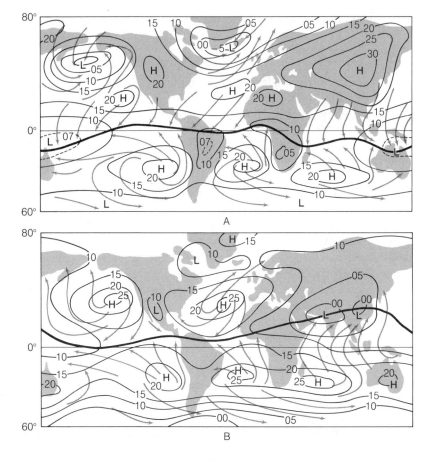

Figure 5-1 Average patterns of sea level winds and pressures over the earth in January (A) and July (B). The lines of constant pressure—that is, the isobars—are labeled with numbers showing how much the pressure exceeds 1,000 mb; for example, the number 20 means that the isobar corresponds to a pressure of 1,020 millibars. (From H. Riehl, *Introduction to the Atmosphere,* 3rd ed., 1978; used with permission of McGraw-Hill, Inc.)

areas dominated by low pressure or where warm, humid air is forced to rise over mountain barriers.

The zone separating the northeast trade winds from the southeast trade winds has mostly low pressure and rising air. This accounts for heavy rainfall in most equatorial regions. Abundant precipitation falls on the windward sides of the mountainous regions that face the oceans but are not under the influence of the sinking air in the semipermanent anticyclones. The windward sides of mountains on tropical islands such as Hawaii get heavy rainfalls. Warm, moist air from over the Indian Ocean blowing

Figure 5-2 Average annual precipitation in inches. (From *Climates of the World*, courtesy of the U.S. Government Printing Office, 1972.)

Precipitation

Under 10 in.

10 to 20 in.

20 to 40 in.

40 to 80 in.

80 to 100 in.

Over 100 in.

north towards the Himalayas in the summer monsoon yields intense rainfall over India and in Southeast Asia.

The belt of relatively low pressure connecting the prevailing cyclones in the north Atlantic and Pacific also has rising air and moderate amounts of precipitation. This is the zone usually occupied by the polar front, separating polar air from tropical air.

GENERAL CIRCULATION MODELS

Scientists have been studying the general circulation of the earth for a long time. The last few decades have also brought increasing research on the atmospheric circulations of other planets. Each atmospheric circulation is unique, but each one conforms to the same physical laws. Knowing the relevant properties of the atmosphere, one can write a series of mathematical equations that quantitatively describes the behavior of the atmosphere and how it changes with time. This set of equations is sometimes called a general circulation model, or GCM.

General circulation models deal with the interrelations of atmospheric pressure, temperature, and other elements; energy transfers by radiation, convection, and other mechanisms; the three-dimensional velocities of air in relation to the relevant forces; the formation of clouds and precipitation; and the interaction of the air with the underlying surfaces.

General circulation models are complex; they deal with huge quantities of data and require very large numbers of calculations. To obtain solutions within a reasonable time, it is necessary to use very fast computers with large memory systems. Computations begin with a specified initial state of the atmosphere; for example, the researcher may start out with an atmosphere perfectly at rest and having a uniform temperature, and then "turn on the sun" and watch the general circulation evolve. After a series of calculations amounting to a simulation of about 300 days, the better models yield patterns of pressure, wind, and temperaure closely resembling actually observed patterns.

General circulation models are being used to assess the effects on the global climate of ocean temperature, of small changes in energy output of the sun, and of increasing atmospheric carbon dioxide. The tentative conclusion, cited in Chapter 2, that a doubling of carbon dioxide would lead to surface warming of about 5°F, was obtained from calculations using a GCM.

Knowing the state of the atmosphere at any initial time, a general circulation model can calculate future atmospheric states. This is the heart of modern weather-forecasting techniques, a subject discussed in more detail in Chapter 6.

WEATHER ABNORMALITIES

Everyone is familiar with the fact that the weather behaves in a fashion that deviates from "normal." Winters may be abnormally cold in some parts of the world and abnormally warm in others. For example, the winter of 1980–1981 was unusually cold in the eastern half of the United States and warmer than normal in the Great Plains states. The droughts discussed in Chapter 4 are extended periods of precipitation much below normal.

These deviations from climatic expectations can be explained in terms of deviations of pressure and wind patterns from the long-term average— in other words, abnormalities in the general circulation. During an average winter, the middle layers of the atmosphere over North America have a trough of pressure over the east and a ridge of high pressure over the west. This pattern governs the flow of air and the location and track of cyclonic systems. If the trough is deeper than normal, the air moving over the eastern states follows a trajectory that comes from frigid Arctic regions. Over the Great Plains, air with an abnormally strong southerly component brings unusual warmth to the Dakotas and Minnesota (as happened in the winter of 1980–1981). Occasionally, the prevailing seasonal pattern of pressure troughs and ridges shifts eastward or westward, shifting temperature and precipitation patterns in the process.

There still is uncertainty and debate about the reasons why the average circulation patterns change from year to year or decade to decade. Some scientists, most notably Jerome Namias, at Scripps Institution of Oceanography in California, have argued that the oceans are the driving factors. He has found that changes in temperature of the ocean surface over large regions of the Pacific have been accompanied by changes of seasonal weather over the United States. Other meteorologists believe that the seasonal and annual variations of atmospheric circulation depend on many additional factors.

LOCAL INFLUENCES ON THE CLIMATE

Local circumstances often exert major influences on the climate, particularly in mountainous terrain, along coast lines, and in large cities. Coastal effects are most noticeable in temperature records and are partly attributable to the sea and land breezes described in Chapter 3. These light winds serve to smooth out temperature extremes.

Regions just downwind of oceans tend to have mild winters and relatively cool summers. Water has a high heat-holding capacity. To warm a cubic foot of water 1°F requires about five times more heat than is needed for the same volume of sand. Heat is readily distributed by convection through a deep layer of water, but it is conducted only slowly through sand, soil, and rock. This accounts, in part, for ocean surface temperatures differing less than land surface temperatures from summer to winter. When cold air passes over warmer water, the large reservoir of available heat raises the air temperature. Conversely, warm air moving over colder water loses heat. In a sense, an ocean serves as a thermostat. Cities downwind of oceans, such as San Francisco, have small temperature changes from winter to summer, while cities in continental interiors have large annual temperature ranges.

Hilly and mountainous terrain can substantially change the distribution of temperatures, winds, and precipitation. Because a barrier forces air to rise, the windward sides of ridges tend to have heavy rains. In places where the winds are humid and consistent, mountain rainfalls are extreme; for example, Mount Waialeale, in Hawaii, averages 460 inches of rain a year.

As the air from which precipitation has fallen subsides on the lee—that is, the sheltered—side of a mountain, cloud formation is inhibited. Consequently, precipitation can be relatively light in the region downwind of a mountain. An example of such a region, sometimes called a "rain shadow," is that on the east side of the Sierra Nevada in California.

In mountainous regions dominated by clear skies, radiation effects are particularly important. At night, losses of heat from the ground and the lowest layers of air lead to a reduction of surface temperatures and the formation of temperature inversions in the lowlands. The cold air, because it is heavier than the surrounding surface air, drains towards lower elevations. Pools of cold air gather in the valleys, particularly in depressions. On a clear winter night when the air is dry, the minimum temperature might be a subfreezing 24°F in the valley bottoms at the same time that the temperature is 33°F along the foothills of surrounding mountains (Figure 5-3). The warm slopes, known as thermal belts, correspond to the upper part of a temperature inversion layer. Frost-sensitive vegetation, such as citrus trees, are more productive on the slopes than in the valleys.

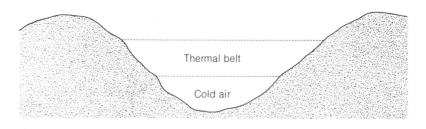

Figure 5-3 Cold air drains into valley bottoms with warmer air in the thermal belts along the slopes.

CITY CLIMATES

As early as 1818, Luke Howard (who, as noted earlier, is responsible for the names we give to clouds) called attention to the fact that central London was warmer than the surrounding rural areas. The situation has not changed. As cities grow, they have increasingly important influences on the local climate. When grass and trees are replaced with pavement and buildings, the disposition of precipitation is drastically altered. In the natural state, some of the rainwater is absorbed by the soil, infiltrates into the ground, and is taken up by the vegetation. In a city environment, much more water runs off into storm sewers and drainage streams, and less is available for evaporation. In some heavily industrialized cities, however, water vapor added to the atmosphere from smoke stacks and cooling towers can increase relative humidity.

In rural environments, water vapor evaporates gradually from the ground, while plant life transpires a great deal of water vapor. These processes add water vapor to the air and also reduce the daytime warming of the air, because heat is consumed in evaporation. When less water is available for evaporation and transpiration, the effects are reduced relative humidities and increased temperatures.

Cities are warmer than the nearby countryside for several other reasons. First of all, the materials used to build roads and buildings absorb a great deal of heat during the daytime. At night they release it through radiation and other processes. In the narrow canyon streets, buildings on opposite sides radiate infrared energy back and forth as well as up to the night sky. The buildings obstruct the winds and, as a result, heat is retained in the area to a greater extent than if the buildings were not there. Finally, in a large city, appreciable heat is generated in, and released from, homes, offices, and factories.

A city is most particularly warmer than its surrounding areas in the winter and at night, during which times it appears as a "heat island" surrounded by cool suburban landscapes (Figure 5-4). Helmut E. Landsberg and his associates at the University of Maryland tracked the climate of the town of Columbia, Maryland, as its population grew from 200 to 20,000 between 1968 and 1975. At the end of this period, the town center had higher temperatures than did the nearby suburban areas. The city itself had warmed by about 14°F by 1974, and warming was continuing as the city enlarged. In extreme cases, large metropolitan areas such as New York or St. Louis can be 20° to 25°F warmer than nonurbanized areas around the city.

Although the air over cities has lower relative humidities, on the average, there tends to be more precipitation—particularly more summer showers and thunderstorms. The buildings act as a barrier that impedes the winds,

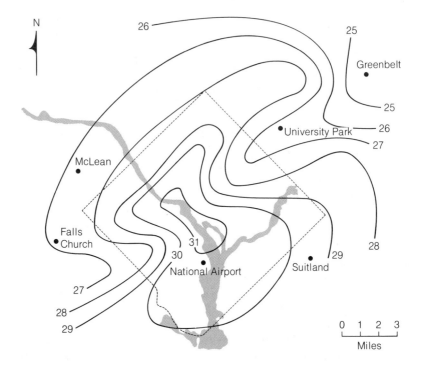

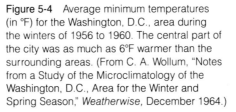

Figure 5-4 Average minimum temperatures (in °F) for the Washington, D.C., area during the winters of 1956 to 1960. The central part of the city was as much as 6°F warmer than the surrounding areas. (From C. A. Wollum, "Notes from a Study of the Microclimatology of the Washington, D.C., Area for the Winter and Spring Season," *Weatherwise,* December 1964.)

causing the air to converge and rise. The higher temperatures of city air with respect to the surroundings contributes to the convection. If the air is sufficiently moist and unstable, cumulus and cumulonimbus clouds occur in, and downwind of, the city.

Finally, we cannot overlook the fact that many human activities in cities—particularly those involving combustion—increase the levels of air pollution. A large urban area on days of fair weather often appears enshrouded in a dome of smoke and dust particles. This dome scatters sunlight, and, from within the city, the sky appears milky rather than blue. Some of the particles can serve as nuclei for cloud droplets and ice crystals, although their importance in influencing temperatures and precipitation is not known.

THE CHANGING GLOBAL CLIMATE

The climate of the earth, as measured by its average surface air temperaure, has been changing virtually since the earth was formed billions of years ago. The deeper one goes into the distant past, the more uncertain and subject to debate is the evidence. Nevertheless, a great deal is known, and more is coming to light as new scientific and engineering techniques are employed to collect and analyze climatic data. Over all time scales, however, climate trends and abnormalities in temperature and precipitation have not been uniform over all parts of the earth.

Geological studies of the structure of the earth and analyses of fossil remains from land and from sea beds tell us a great deal about ancient climates. Over the last million years or so, the planet experienced a series of ice ages lasting about 100,000 years and separated by relatively warm interglacial periods lasting about 10,000 years. The term *ice age* is used to identify an abnormally cold period during which polar ice sheets extended to about middle latitudes. Typically, the limit of ice cover over North America was south of Chicago; over Europe, south of Berlin.

The last glacial age, called the Wisconsin, ended about 10,000 years ago. At the time of the glacial maximum, 18,000 years ago, average air temperatures in the middle latitudes of the Northern Hemisphere were 10° to 15°F colder than they are today. Sea level was about 300 feet lower than now, because a greater fraction of the earth's water was in the form of ice on the continents.

Over the last 10,000 years, the earth has been in a mild interglacial interval. Historical records of human experiences, analyses of tree rings from old trees and timbers (Figure 5-5), the study of pollen from the past,

Figure 5-5   The widths of the rings of certain trees are good indicators of the climate. Each ring represents one year's growth, which depends to an important extent on available water. (Photo by Bob Broder, courtesy of Laboratory of Tree-Ring Research, University of Arizona, Tucson.)

and meteorological data over the last few centuries show that even this interval has had relatively small but important climatic vibrations.

From 5600 to 2500 B.C., the earth was warm—4–6°F warmer than now—and moist. This period has been named the "Climatic Optimum" because atmospheric conditions were so favorable for humans, animals, and plant life.

The four centuries A.D. 1500–1900, the "Little Ice Age," were relatively dry and cool in the Northern Hemisphere; temperatures were 2° to 4°F lower than they are today. During this period, sea ice extended toward the equator and glaciers advanced as far south as the Alps—a fact well documented by paintings and etchings of the time. (See Chapter 13.)

From about 1880 to 1940, the surface air temperature averaged over most of the Northern Hemisphere increased by about 2°F (Figure 5-6). This warming was accompanied by a reduction of sea ice, a retreat of glaciers up the valleys they occupy, a small rise of sea level, and a lengthening of the agricultural growing season, particularly at colder latitudes. From about 1940 to the middle 1960s, average global temperature decreased about 1°F; since then there has been a gradual warming.

Many hypotheses have been offered to account for the variations of climate that have occurred. Changes over periods of hundreds of millions of years can be ascribed to shifts of the continents over the face of the

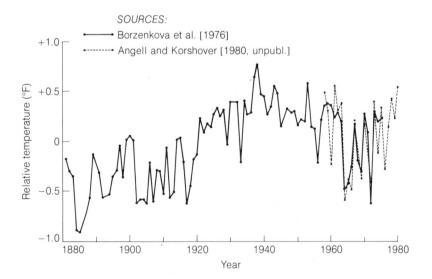

Figure 5-6   Variations of the estimated air temperature near the earth's surface over that part of the Northern Hemisphere north of 15°N latitude. (Plotted by J. Murray Mitchell, Jr., NOAA.)

planet. The modern view of the earth is that the continents are composed of relatively low-density materials and that the continents are floating on higher-density material at the earth's interior. In the process, the continents drift with respect to one another; for example, Africa and South America appear to have once been together. The east coast of South America and the west coast of Africa can be fitted together almost as if they were pieces of a jigsaw puzzle. As the continents have changed shapes and locations on the earth, there have been changes in the general circulation of the atmosphere and of the climate.

Climate variations over periods ranging from about 10,000 to 100,000 years apparently are caused by cyclical alterations of the earth's orbit and the orientation of its axis. This hypothesis, first discussed in the middle of the nineteenth century, was developed in detail in the 1920s by the Serbian scientist Milutin Milankovitch, who calculated that changes in the pattern of solar radiation intercepted by the earth should lead to cycles of climate of about 20,000, 40,000, and 95,000 years. Recent research has tended to support the validity of these findings, and, according to the Milankovitch theory, the earth is now in a slow cooling trend leading to a temperature minimum, which will occur in about a thousand years.

Various explanations have been advanced to explain climatic fluctuations over intervals of from tens to hundreds of years. A group of so-called nonastronomical hypotheses ascribe changes in climate to terrestrial events, such as volcanic eruptions that emit gases and particles into the atmosphere. The evidence does show that a massive eruption can add enough aerosols to the stratosphere to cause minor cooling in the lower atmosphere, but there is little support for the view that this can lead to an ice age— even a "little" one.

Astronomical hypotheses for climate change have received a great deal of attention for some time. The scientific literature contains many contributions seeking to show that weather and climate are related to sunspots, large, dark spots on the face of the sun. Sunspots average about 25,000 miles in diameter and change in number from year to year. Particularly large spots were observed by the naked eye and recorded in China at least 15 centuries ago, but Galileo is regarded as having first observed sunspots telescopically in about A.D. 1610.

From about 1645 to 1715, the sun was almost devoid of sunspots (Figure 5-7). A British expert on the sun, E. W. Maunder, is reported to have been the first person to call attention to this 70-year interval, which is thus called the "Maunder Minimum." The man who coined this name, John A. Eddy, of the National Center for Atmospheric Research in Colorado, has pointed out that the minimum occurred during the Little Ice Age. Whether changes in solar radiation associated with the near absence of sunspots caused the prolonged cold period is still the subject of speculation and debate.

76

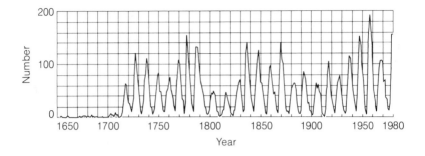

Figure 5-7   Occurrences of sunspots, 1650–1980. (Data by J. A. Eddy, courtesy of NCAR/NSF.)

A much-discussed feature of the sunspot record is the well-established, roughly 11-year cycle of maxima and minima that have occurred since about 1715. There also is an associated 22-year cycle that appears as changes in the magnetic fields associated with the sunspots. In general, the correlations between sunspot frequency and elements of the weather and climate are not sufficiently high to be convincing. Most important, no one has yet proposed a plausible physical mechanism by which solar emissions associated with sunspots can influence the weather and climate. For this reason, hypotheses proposing a cause-and-effect relationship are viewed with skepticism by most atmospheric scientists.

CLIMATE PREDICTIONS

There is strong evidence that increases in atmospheric carbon dioxide can lead to global warming of the lower atmosphere (see Chapter 2). In some circumstances, long-lasting particles in the atmosphere can lead to global cooling. Following the eruptions of Krakatoa in 1883 and Mount Agung in 1963, stratospheric particles caused surface air temperatures to be reduced by several tenths of a degree Fahrenheit for one or two years. To date, emissions from Mount St. Helens have been too small to cause a detectable temperaure change over the globe. On the other hand, the explosion on April 4, 1982, of the El Chichón volcano in Mexico threw into the upper atmosphere at least ten times more sulfur dioxide and other substances than did Mount St. Helens. The resulting stratospheric aerosols are expected to cause cooling effects similar to those observed after the eruptions of Krakatoa and Agung.

Over the last few decades, those who search for frightening trends have been able to piece together evidence for their scenarios. In the forties, they were tormented by the thought of rising global temperatures, widespread flooding, and other natural disasters. By the seventies, talk of overheating began to be replaced by talk of overcooling. Drowning became less of a threat, but freezing became a new concern. Cautious scientists, while examining the causes and consequences of rising and falling temperatures, warned about the difficulty of predicting future climates, but the headline writers usually found the words to make the possible appear to be the probable.

Press stories of possible climatic catastrophes are particularly eye-catching because of the opinions of some experts that the variations over the last century might have been a result of human activity. First it was suggested that burning fossil fuels led to increased atmospheric carbon dioxide and global warming. But after 1940, the planet began to cool even as carbon dioxide continued to increase. Certain writers suggested that increases in atmospheric smoke and dust were causing enough cooling to overcome the CO_2 effect and that the earth might be heading for an ice age. Unfortunately, we still do not know enough to explain satisfactorily what has been happening to the climate over the last few decades.

What will the climate be like over the next decade or two? Many prophets—scientific and otherwise—are making predictions, but there is no scientific basis for prediction other than the use of the past to determine a likely range of future conditions. Flipping a coin to determine whether it will be warmer or colder five years from now—heads, colder; tails, warmer—may be as good as asking an expert to decide.

This is not to say we are totally ignorant about the possibilities for the longer term. The best available information indicates that a very large increase of atmospheric carbon dioxide is likely to lead to appreciable warming. The consequences of such a result are so great that it is vital that we engage in a vigorous program of research to determine the facts and clear away the uncertainties as quickly as possible.

CHAPTER 6
Weather Forecasting

For many people, the weather is an inevitability that must be accepted. To these people, stormy days differ from fair ones only in that, on the former, raincoats and umbrellas come out of the closet. But for farmers, fliers, sailors, and many other people, their lives and livelihoods critically depend on the beneficence of the atmosphere. In order to survive and thrive, these people must try to anticipate the weather and optimize their activities accordingly. This requires that attempts be made to forecast the weather as accurately as possible and as far into the future as necessary.

Anyone who regularly follows the progression of weather systems can develop some skill as a forecaster. An observer of atmospheric pressure, cloud types, and wind velocities can often predict accurately, a day or two in advance, the onset of stormy weather. Simple procedures based on observations at a single location are most effective in middle latitudes during the cold seasons, when the weather is dominated by large, slowly changing anticyclones and cyclones. But sometimes the storms fail to follow the usual sequence of development or do not move along the normal tracks. Sometimes a storm may stagnate or even reverse its direction of travel.

Times of occurrence and locations of short-lived events such as thunderstorms, hailstorms, and tornadoes cannot be predicted with any accuracy by observing conditions early in the day before clouds have begun to form. To predict these storms skillfully, weather maps are needed that depict the three-dimensional state of the atmosphere in detail. These maps must include vertical soundings of the atmosphere at many places over the forecasting region, showing how pressure, temperature, humidity, and wind vary with height. Such information indicates whether the atmosphere is stable or unstable and permits estimates of the likelihood of thunderstorms and the attendant violent weather.

There are many ways to predict the weather, and some are better than others. But judging the value of any forecasting procedure is not always easy.

PREDICTION IS EASY

If you are satisfied being right about half the time, it is simple to predict whether or not it will rain tomorrow or a year or even a century from now, and there are many ways to do it. One way is to flip a coin—the result is worthless meteorologically, but it might help you make a weather-related decision.

There are other, more imaginative, but equally unworthy prediction methods that get more attention than they deserve. One brand of weather prophecy makes use of the positions of planets in a form of atmospheric astrology called astrometeorology. Some people examine the behavior of caterpillars, spiders, or goldfish. There are countless weather sayings relating to animal behavior. In *Weather Proverbs*, published in 1883 by H. H. C. Dunwoody, one finds: "When the finch chirps, rain follows"; "When the thrush sings at sunset, a fair day will follow"; and "When summer birds take their flight, summer goes with them." Most weather sayings are of little value for forecasting, but some that relate the color of the clouds or the sky to the next day's weather do have validity.

In many places you can be right most of the time by merely predicting for tomorrow whatever happened today. This is known as "persistence forecasting." It is particularly successful in arid regions, where it seldom rains, and in very wet regions, where it rains very often.

Whenever you read about weather forecasting, it is important to recognize that with virtually no knowledge of how the atmosphere works, you can sometimes predict weather events in the distant future with a high percentage of success. The technique involves the use of climatic statistics.

Consider the following example: Past records show that in Los Angeles, out of any 62 July and August days, it usually rains once (Appendix I). Therefore, by merely predicting no rain in Los Angeles for any particular day in any July or August 1990, you can expect to be right about 98 percent of the time.

Obviously, you do not have to be a trained meteorologist to achieve such impressive results. Anyone having access to the climatic data could do just as well. Such data can also be used to predict weather conditions in places where rain is fairly plentiful. On the average, Chicago has rain on 9 days during July. If you are asked to forecast the weather for July 15, 1990, you may be wise to predict that rain will occur, even though the chance of rain is only about 30 percent for that day. If it rained on July 14 or July 16, you might say, "The forecast was not perfect, but it was a real accomplishment—it only missed by one day although it was made so many years in advance!"

Such an observation tends to grossly overestimate the ability of the forecaster. If there is a 30 percent chance of rain on one day, there is a 66 percent chance of rain on one or more of three successive days. This is strictly the case if the probability of rain on each day is independent of the probability of rain on the other days. Therefore, in Chicago, rain is likely on July 15, 1990, or on the preceding or following day.

The point to remember is that knowing nothing about the present state of the atmosphere or caterpillars or planets, one can use climatic data to predict the chances of rain at any place at any time in the future. Such predictions are valuable because they are correct more often than a pure guess or a coin flip would be. They are particularly useful in anticipating the weather in a distant place that has a climate different from the familiar hometown climate.

Meteorologists expect the accuracy of forecasts to be higher than could be achieved by the use of persistence methods or climatic statistics alone. Such accuracy indicates forecasting skill. A good forecaster should succeed, at least some of the time, in anticipating exactly on which day in July and August rain will fall in Los Angeles.

COMPUTERS

The history of meteorology includes a number of individuals known to have been unusually skilled weather forecasters. Apparently they were able to recognize, on the basis of past experience, how pressure and frontal patterns would change over succeeding days. This is speculation because it appears that outstanding forecasters, such as the legendary Charles Mitchell, who worked for the U.S. Weather Bureau from 1904 to 1950, could not adequately account for their success or teach others how to achieve it. Contemporary meteorologists have the assistance of high-speed computers to process atmospheric measurements, analyze weather maps and use mathematical models of the atmosphere to calculate future states of the atmosphere.

Before computer-based techniques became available in the 1950s, most forecasts were essentially extrapolations of past events. A meteorologist would examine a series of weather maps and observe the evolution of high- and low-pressure areas and the development and movements of fronts. Maps were scrutinized for regions where atmospheric pressure had been rising or falling rapidly. Widespread cloudiness, rain, or snow were taken as evidence of ascending air motions and the possibility of an incipient cyclone. The *art* of weather forecasting consisted of the subjective weighing of these many factors. The *science* of weather forecasting, on the other hand, employs mathematical models of the atmosphere.

The mathematical models used to predict the weather are essentially the same as the ones constituting the general circulation models discussed in Chapter 5. Because of the complex interactions in the atmosphere, the equations involved have to be solved by techniques mathematicians call

numerical methods. For this reason, the modern methods used by meteorologists are called numerical weather prediction methods. In essence,
they start with a known initial state of the atmosphere and calculate changes
that will occur within a short period, generally about 10 minutes. This
yields a new set of conditions that are used to calculate changes over succeeding brief periods as far into the future as seems to be reasonable.

Unfortunately, errors that enter the model at the outset, possibly from
incorrect observations, tend to be amplified with time. After a forecast
period of a week or more, the errors can be so large as to make the calculations of future atmospheric states of little value.

Numerical weather prediction requires a detailed and accurate knowledge of atmospheric conditions at the beginning of the forecast period.
The necessary data are obtained mostly by means of a global network of
rawinsonde stations (Figure 6-1). The rawinsonde is an instrument carried

Figure 6-1   A rawinsonde about to be released. When the
balloon breaks (at an altitude of perhaps 100,000 feet), a small
parachute opens and lowers the rawinsonde to the ground.
(Courtesy of NOAA.)

Figure 6-2 Clouds observed on July 10, 1979, by infrared sensors on geostationary weather satellite. (Courtesy of National Earth Satellite Service/NOAA.)

aloft, to as high as 100,000 feet, on a balloon. As it rises, the device measures pressure, temperature, and humidity, and transmits the information by radio to a receiver on the ground. Tracking the instrument can also provide wind velocities. Rawinsonde stations are spaced a few hundred miles apart over the land areas of the world, particularly in the more advanced countries. There are about 110 stations in North America. Balloons are released twice a day, at 30 to 45 minutes before both midnight and noon Greenwich Mean Time (that is, at about 6:30 A.M. and 6:30 P.M. EST).

Weather satellites came into use in April 1960 with the launch of the first Television and Infrared Observation Satellite (TIROS). Over subsequent years, they have been used increasingly to make observations of temperatures, humidities, wind velocities, and the distribution of clouds showing the location and size of storm systems (Figure 6-2). These measurements are particularly valuable over the oceans, where observations can be made by only a few rawinsonde stations located on islands or ships.

Data obtained by rawinsondes and satellites are combined with observations made at weather stations on land and at sea. In accordance with international agreements drawn up by the World Meteorological Organization, weather data from all over the world are transmitted to data centers in Washington, D.C., Moscow, and Melbourne, Australia and to national weather offices all over the world.

An enormous quantity of weather information is generated every day. For example, a single satellite can transmit as many as 2 million bits of data per second. Fortunately, large modern computers can handle such mountains of information and carry out the calculation of future states of the atmosphere in reasonable amounts of time. As general circulation models become even more realistic simulations of the real atmosphere than they are now, computers even larger than those that exist today will be needed.

LONG-TERM PREDICTION

The amount of information needed to make a weather prediction depends on the period of the forecast. The best technique for predicting what is likely to happen in ten minutes, is to observe present conditions and extrapolate—that is, to look out the window. This procedure is also valid in many circumstances for making a forecast for a period of an hour or two. But in these cases, it is necessary to know the state of the surrounding atmosphere to about a hundred miles from the point of forecast. A radar set may be used to observe the location, size, and intensity of small-scale phenomena such as thunderstorms (Figure 6-3).

Prediction by means of a numerical model of the general pattern of air motions in the middle atmosphere more than a day in advance requires data over an entire hemisphere. Beyond about three days, the oceans begin to affect the weather and must be taken into account. For forecasts more than a week in advance, the mathematical models require initial observations of the entire atmosphere to a height of 100,000 feet and the ocean to a depth of about 30 feet. Only by means of satellites can these lofty observational goals ever be achieved.

Numerical models are used to calculate future attributes of the atmosphere, such as patterns of pressure, wind, and temperature at many levels in the atmosphere; fields of vertical air motion; probability of rain and snow; and the quantity of precipitation.

In the United States, the National Meteorological Center in Washington, D.C., is responsible for collecting up-to-date observations, constructing weather maps of many types, making numerical weather predictions, and distributing the results throughout the United States and abroad. Every day, about 500 weather maps and charts are transmitted via telephone lines and radio to facsimile recorders that print the maps in government weather stations, universities, and private organizations. In addition, weather

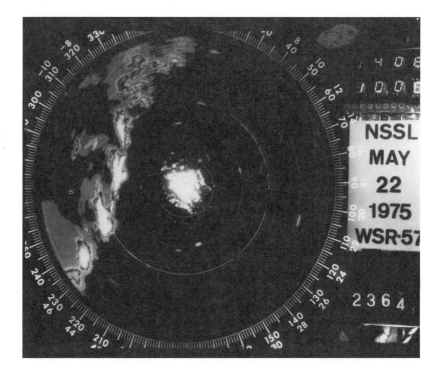

Figure 6-3 A nearby north–south line of severe thunderstorms approaching from the west, observed on a radarscope at the National Severe Storms Laboratory at Norman, Oklahoma. The circular markers are in 25-mile increments. (Photo by R. Doviak, courtesy of NSSL/NOAA.)

observations taken hourly (or even more frequently during threatening weather) at airport, city, and other stations are distributed by teletype networks. These data are of particular value for aircraft operators and for others interested in rapidly changing weather events.

A meteorologist predicting maximum and minimum temperatures, precipitation, and winds at any location uses the outputs of numerical prediction models. In addition, the forecaster must take into account how the atmosphere is changing between the periods of the calculated prognostic maps, as well as local weather peculiarities associated with terrain.

FORECASTING SKILL

The accuracy of numerical weather prediction models can be measured by comparing calculated future pressure patterns with those that actually occurred, as Frederick G. Shuman, director of the National Meteorological

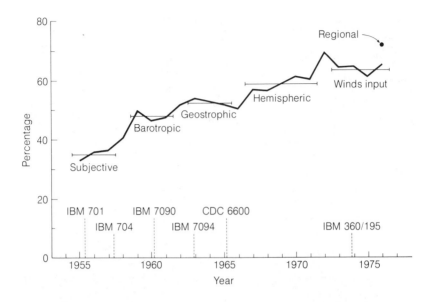

Figure 6-4 Record of the average skill of the National Meteorological Center in predicting the pressure patterns occurring 36 hours later in the middle atmosphere over North America. In this analysis, the term "skill" is a calculated index of forecast accuracy: Zero skill means the predicted weather chart is worthless; 100 would indicate a virtually perfect forecast. Horizontal lines identify time spans during which the indicated models were used to make the forecasts. The successively more powerful computers used are indicated along the horizontal axis at the years they were introduced. (From F. G. Shuman, "Numerical Weather Prediction," *Bulletin of American Meteorological Society,* January 1978.)

Center, has done (Figure 6-4). The graph shows the level of skill at forecasting the pattern of pressure at altitudes corresponding to the 500-millibar pressure level. The graph also shows that as new numerical prediction models (barotropic, geostrophic, and so on) were introduced, forecasting skill increased. It also names the newer, larger, and faster computers that were introduced to handle the increasingly sophisticated numerical prediction models. The IBM 360/195, introduced in 1974, is about 600 times faster than the IBM 701 used in the middle fifties.

According to Shuman, three- to six-day forecasts of atmospheric circulation are being made much more accurately today than they were in the middle fifties. Forecasts of precipitation and temperature maxima and minima at the ground have improved over the last few decades, but not as much as the predictions of pressure patterns in the free atmosphere have.

In many instances, the percent of correct forecasts is a poor indication of forecasting skill, but a *change* in the percent of correct forecasts can indicate whether meteorologists are developing greater skills. A study of forecasting accuracy in Chicago indicates that weather forecasters have become more skillful, particularly since the introduction of numerical prediction techniques (Figure 6-5).

According to a statement issued in 1979 by the American Meteorological Society, the quality of weather forecasts in the Northern Hemisphere can be summarized as follows:

For periods up to 48 hours: There is considerable skill in forecasts of cloudiness, air quality, temperature, and precipitation when the weather is dominated by large-scale weather systems. The general area of severe storms—such as thunderstorms and tornadoes—can be predicted up to 24 hours in advance but the exact location of the storms cannot be predicted. Once their formation has been detected, their future positions can be predicted accurately an hour or two in advance.

For periods of 2 to 5 days: "Daily temperature forecasts of moderate skill and usefulness are possible. Precipitation forecasts at an equivalent level of skill, can be made to 3 days." Precipitation forecasts 4 to 5 days in the future are only slightly better than can be achieved by means of climatological techniques.

For periods of 5 days to 1 month: "Average temperature conditions can be predicted with some skill, particularly in the 6–10 day period. There is slight skill in forecasting precipitation amounts for the 6–10 day period but skill for longer periods is marginal. Weak-to-week forecasts beyond 10 days have not demonstrated skill."

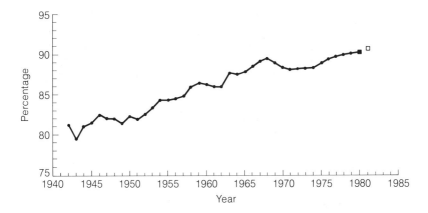

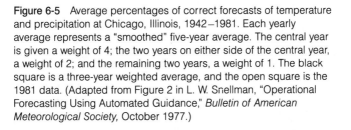

Figure 6-5   Average percentages of correct forecasts of temperature and precipitation at Chicago, Illinois, 1942–1981. Each yearly average represents a "smoothed" five-year average. The central year is given a weight of 4; the two years on either side of the central year, a weight of 2; and the remaining two years, a weight of 1. The black square is a three-year weighted average, and the open square is the 1981 data. (Adapted from Figure 2 in L. W. Snellman, "Operational Forecasting Using Automated Guidance," *Bulletin of American Meteorological Society,* October 1977.)

For periods of more than 1 month: "A minimal skill exists in seasonal outlooks."

The quality of forecasts in tropical regions and in the Southern Hemisphere is lower than in the middle latitudes of the Northern Hemisphere, where there are more observations and more is known about the weather systems that prevail.*

DISSEMINATION OF WEATHER FORECASTS

Most people keep abreast of the weather by way of radio, television, newspapers, and, particularly on stormy days, telephone. In the United States, there are about one billion calls a year for National Weather Service information. In New York City alone, there are about 1600 lines serving people who dial the weather service number.

Continuous broadcasts of weather forecasts are available to anyone who lives within range of a NOAA Weather Radio station. In 1975, the National Oceanic and Atmospheric Administration began transmitting weather information—in one of three frequency bands near 162 megahertz—directly from National Weather Service offices. Small, relatively inexpensive radios have been designed to receive these broadcasts. About 15 million receivers are currently in use in the United States. The radios are particularly valuable in areas that experience violent weather events such as tornadoes, hurricanes, and flash floods.

Most television news programs include a segment on the weather. A 15-minute show, AM *Weather,* concerned primarily with aviation weather, is produced by the National Weather Service and distributed to about 200 stations in the Public Broadcasting System. In 1982 *The Weather Channel* went on the air. It is a 24-hour cable-television operation developed by John Coleman, its president. From its headquarters in Atlanta, Georgia, the station offers a continuous stream of weather observations, forecasts, advisories, and features. The program uses modern and sophisticated observational and graphic techniques and employs a large staff of trained meteorologists.

GOVERNMENT AND PRIVATE FORECASTERS

The nature and value of forecasts depend to a significant extent on the ability, commitment, and responsibilities of the meteorologists who make them. The National Weather Service is charged primarily with supplying forecasts to the general public and is particularly concerned with violent

---

*From the *Bulletin of American Meteorological Society,* Dec. 1979, pp. 1453–1454.

weather that threatens life and property. Forecasts of hurricane development and motion are made by the National Hurricane Center, in Miami, Florida. Forecasts of severe thunderstorms, hailstorms, and tornadoes are the responsibility of the National Severe Storms Forecast Center, in Kansas City, Missouri.

The National Weather Service is obliged, by current federal statutes, to furnish certain specialized weather service to pilots, mariners, and some agricultural interests. For example, during periods of potential frost damage, the citrus growers of Florida get special attention; storm warnings are issued on a regular basis to fishermen and others who operate boats and ships. In 1982, the federal government, in a move to reduce expenditures, was considering a reduction of weather services to agriculture, aviation, and other specialized interests that have traditionally received them at no direct cost. The federal government does not provide weather services tailored to the requirements of such weather-sensitive interests as the construction industry, truckers and railroaders, electric and gas companies, health and sports resorts, and smelting and refining companies.

People or groups with special weather concerns should not rely solely on the general forecasts of temperature, winds, and precipitation distributed by the National Weather Service. The services of a skilled consulting meteorologist could help maximize benefits when the weather is favorable and minimize losses when it is unfavorable. Such an individual, knowing how the weather affects a particular enterprise, can give the kind of advice that is needed. In addition, a first-rate consulting meteorologist keeps the client's welfare in mind 24 hours a day. As in all fields, some persons give better service than others. The American Meteorological Society (45 Beacon Street, Boston, MA 02108) has a list of persons who have met the requirements for designation as certified consulting meteorologist.

CHAPTER 7
Changing the Weather

For the most part, we accept the weather as it comes, and, by predicting its future course, attempt to take advantage of it when possible and protect ourselves when necessary. But many people have sought to change the weather. They have prayed, sung, rung church bells, danced, flung stones and spears at the heavens, and fired cannons and rockets toward the sky in attempts to bring rain, calm the wind, or stop lightning. These actions may not have affected the weather, but they were not entirely without benefit—they satisfied a need to do something in the face of adversity and kept people from feeling totally helpless.

To an important extent, farmers have been successful in modifying the effects of atmosphere in its lowest layer, the one in which vegetation grows. They irrigate in times of dry weather; they grow rows of trees to reduce wind damage; they employ orchard heaters, wind machines, and other devices to raise temperatures to protect berries and citrus from killing frosts.

In a sense, we all control the weather. Specifically, we create our own atmospheres by living and working in buildings that are heated and cooled. Let the snowy blasts of winter or the torrential storms of summer come: Within our thermostatically and hygrometrically controlled cocoons, we are comfortably insulated from the weather. Moreover, if we don't like the weather in one place, we can move to another place.

Greenhouse horticulture does for tomatoes, cucumbers, and many other fruits, vegetables, and flowers what air-conditioned living does for people. The shelter of glass protects the plants from winds and excessive rainfall and allows careful control of the growing environment. Some futurists see entire cities similarly sheltered by huge plastic bubbles, within which the quality of the air can be maintained at any desirable level. This may happen some day—but not for several generations at least. The engineering problems of such an enterprise are enormous.

The notions of cities on the moon or in giant spaceships also are far ahead of the times. It is fun to speculate about such space-age communities and to design them, but they are not likely to come to pass in the next 100 years. Maintaining a few tens or hundreds of people in an orbiting satellite would certainly be within the realm of possibility were the necessary billions of dollars available, but to dream about solving the earth's population problems by going into space is to run away from reality. The earth is our home, as it will be for our children's grandchildren. We must live with the earth's weather or learn how to change it.

SCIENTIFIC BASIS FOR WEATHER MODIFICATION

In Chapter 5, we noted how the weather and climate of cities are being modified inadvertently by human activities. Over the last few decades, atmospheric scientists have devoted a great deal of effort in searching for ways to alter the weather purposefully, an activity often called "weather modification." In particular, there has been a great deal of research on ways to dissipate clouds, increase rain and snow, and reduce the intensity of violent storms.

The foundations for current attempts at weather modification were set in the 1930s. A Scandinavian meteorologist, Tor Bergeron, expanded the findings of Alfred Wegener, a German, who in 1911 reported that when ice crystals and water droplets coexist at subfreezing temperatures, the ice crystals grow as the droplets evaporate. (See Chapter 4.)

In the mid 1940s, Vincent J. Schaefer, at the General Electric Laboratories in Schenectady, New York, found that ice crystals could be produced in a supercooled cloud by dropping small pellets of dry ice (solid carbon dioxide) into it. This process is known as *cloud seeding*. Dry ice has a temperature of about $-108°F$, and, as the pellets fall through a cloud, they cool the air to less than $-40°F$, at which temperatures ice crystals can form in the absence of ice nuclei. At cloud temperatures below $32°F$, the ice crystals can survive and grow as supercooled droplets evaporate. Bernard Vonnegut, who (along with Schaefer) was working with Nobel laureate Irving Langmuir, discovered that a smoke composed of minute silver iodide particles can produce great quantities of ice crystals at temperatures below about $23°F$.

A great deal of research in many countries has developed devices and techniques for seeding supercooled clouds with ice nuclei (Figure 7-1). In addition, there have been many investigations of methods for modifying so-called warm clouds, that is, clouds with temperatures above $32°F$.

The team of scientists at the General Electric Laboratories showed that if substances such as finely divided dry ice or silver iodide were "seeded" into a thin, supercooled layer of clouds, a hole could be produced as the seeded area dissipated (Figure 7-2). The seeding agent caused ice particles that grew large enough to fall out of a cloud in the form of a snow shower.

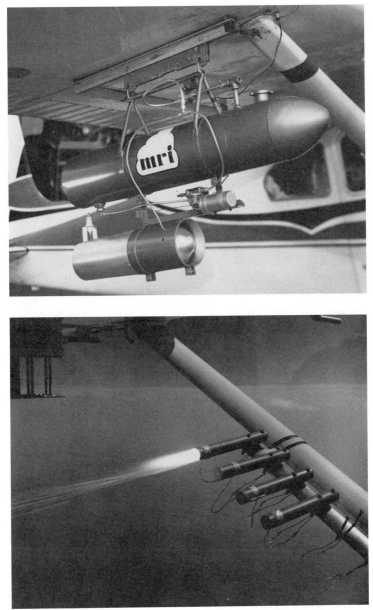

Figure 7-1 A. Silver iodide generator mounted under the wing of a light airplane. The upper cylinder holds a solution of silver iodide in acetone. The highly flammable liquid is sprayed into the burning chamber at the bottom. (Courtesy of Meteorology Research, Inc.) B. Pyrotechnic cloud-seeding devices mounted on wing strut of light single-engine airplane. Each unit contains 40 grams of silver iodide, which is released as smoke in a 5-minute burn. (Photo by Thomas J. Henderson, Atmospherics Incorporated.)

Figure 7-2 Racetrack-shaped hole cut into a supercooled cloud by dry ice pellets dropped from an airplane. (Courtesy of Vincent J. Schaefer.)

Many experiments have sought to establish whether seeding can increase or decrease rain, snow, and hail. Also, there has been widespread use of cloud seeding on an operational, rather than experimental, basis in the United States and many other countries on all continents. Such operations usually are conducted in hope that the seeding might increase precipitation for agriculture and hydroelectric power production, alleviate the effects of droughts, or reduce hail damage to vegetation. Unfortunately, most of these programs have been carried out in such a way that it is impossible to know if the seeding brought about the desired results.

Although there is no doubt that supercooled clouds can often be converted to ice crystals and caused to dissipate, progress in developing effective weather modification technologies has been disappointingly slow.

CLEARING FOGS OVER AIRPORTS

The clearing of supercooled fogs over airports by means of ice-nuclei seeding is a proven technology and is used regularly in various countries. The term *technology* is used here to mean a method of achieving a predictable, economically feasible result. The seeding procedures can be improved, but the ones used now are effective to the extent of costing less than the benefits they produce.

Fogs at temperatures warmer than 32°F, the most common type of fog, can be caused to evaporate by raising the air temperature. This idea was put into practice in England during World War II to make it possible for Royal Air Force planes to land after returning from combat missions. Fifteen airfields were equipped with a thermal fog dissipation system called "Fog, Intensive Dispersal of" (FIDO). Each system consisted of a series of perforated pipes along the runways, through which aviation fuel was pumped and burned. From November 1943 to the end of the war, over 2,500 aircraft carrying about 10,000 airmen landed with the aid of FIDO. Following the war, extensive tests were made of FIDO in the United States. According to B. A. Silverman and A. I. Weinstein, it was concluded in 1953 that "an effective system was too expensive to warrant routine use by commercial aviation."[*] But since the late 1950s, there has been considerable interest in the United States and France in the use of heated air to disperse fogs over airports. In 1970 a sophisticated thermal fog-dissipation system known as Turboclair was installed at Orly Airport in Paris (Figure 7-3). Jet engines in pits along the edge of a runway generate streams of hot air that cause fogs to evaporate. This allows landings and takeoffs that would otherwise have not been possible. Aviation authorities in other countries are not yet convinced that the technique is worth the cost.

INCREASING RAIN AND SNOW

A large fraction of the cloud-seeding programs around the world have been carried out with the intent of increasing rain and snow. Evidence suggests that in certain circumstances it should be possible to cause 10 to 30 percent more precipitation than would have occurred without seeding. Experiments in winter over the Colorado Mountains and in Israel and Tasmania have given reasons for optimism that this can be done. But there have been many experiments with negative or inconclusive results. In the view of many experts, it has not yet been convincingly shown that rain or snow can be augmented enough—at least 10 percent—to be of significant benefit in agriculture and hydroelectric power production.

Uncertainties about the effectiveness of cloud seeding result from our inability to predict accurately how much rain would occur if there were no seeding and from the highly variable nature of rain and snow. It is difficult to determine a 10-percent change in precipitation when normal variations are very much greater. As more is learned about the details of rain and snow processes, it should be possible to conduct more informative experiments and operations.

---

[*]B. A. Silverman and A. I. Weinstein, "Fog," in *Weather and Climate Modification*, W. N. Hess, ed., John Wiley & Sons, 1974.

Figure 7-3 The Turboclair installation at Orly Airport, Paris, France. (Photo by Jean-J. Moreau, Cliché, Aeroport de Paris.)

SUPPRESSING HAIL

The same reservations about the effects of cloud seeding on rain and snow apply to an even greater degree in judging whether or not cloud seeding can reduce the fall of damaging hail. Ice-nuclei seeding is assumed to cause the formation of very many small hailstones, which melt as they fall, in place of fewer but larger damaging ones that would normally have formed.

For more than 15 years, meteorologists in the Soviet Union have been claiming that ice-nuclei seeding of potential hailstorms has reduced hail damage to grapes and other crops by 60 to 90 percent. The Soviets employ unique cloud-seeding methods: They inject ice nuclei into thunderstorms by means of rockets or artillery shells (Figure 7-4).

In the United States, hail damage to grains, fruits, and vegetables amounts to more than $700 million a year; an effective hail-suppression technique would be most welcome. But American experts tend to be skeptical about the Soviet claims. In Colorado, from 1972 to 1974 the National Center for Atmospheric Research tested the Soviet hailstorm-seeding procedures, failing to show that hail could be reduced. Unfortunately, the seeding techniques used in the USSR could not be replicated exactly.

A joint Swiss-French-Italian hail-seeding experiment was conducted in Switzerland from 1976 to 1981 to test the effects of Soviet rocket-seeding procedures. In 1982, it was reported that the results did not confirm Soviet claims. Most experts outside the Soviet Union agree that existing techniques of hail suppression have not been shown to be effective. Cloud seeding for this purpose is even more of a gamble than is the use of cloud seeding for rainfall augmentation. In some cases, cloud seeding might *decrease* rainfall or *increase* hail. In theory, if too many ice crystals are

Figure 7-4   Soviet rockets and launch system for antihall project. The projectiles usually contain lead iodide that is released as a smoke in the supercooled regions of the clouds. (Photo by Thomas J. Henderson, Atmospherics Incorporated.)

produced in a supercooled cloud (a condition known as overseeding), precipitation is inhibited. In some cases, ice-nuclei seeding of a thunderstorm might initiate the hail-formation process and cause an increase in hail. The evidence for such results is not conclusive, but there is a real possibility that in some circumstance, cloud seeding might aggravate a problem of too little rain or too much hail that it was meant to solve.

Questions about the effects of seeding on areas downwind of the so-called target area cannot yet be answered satisfactorily. Some people assume that an increase in precipitation in one area must mean a decrease somewhere else, but the matter is not nearly so simple. If seeding affects the precipitation at all, it could do so over a large region; there is some suggestion of increases and decreases downwind of the primary target areas of seeding operations. Unfortunately, the evidence is difficult to interpret and is the subject of considerable debate.

WEAKENING HURRICANES

In theory, heavy ice-nuclei seeding of the clouds in a hurricane could lead to changes in the pattern of atmospheric pressure in the storm and to a reduction of maximum wind speeds. If this could be done, the size of the storm-induced waves and the surge of ocean water over coastlines could be reduced. The consequences would be a decrease in storm damage and in the number of injuries and fatalities. The results of two hurricane-seeding experiments in August 1969 tend to support this hypothesis, but there have not been enough tests to allow a conclusion.

Before seeding hurricanes approaching populated areas, it is essential to learn more about the possible consequences. There is some concern that seeding might affect a hurricane's future path. Such a change following seeding might be perceived as having been caused by seeding and lead to lawsuits. More experiments need to be carried out over the open oceans.

Unfortunately, very few hurricanes occur in regions that can be reached by seeding airplanes and yet are far from inhabited land. Proposals that experiments be conducted in the western Pacific were rejected by the Japanese government. It is unlikely that in the near future there will be an effective technology for weakening hurricanes.

SOCIAL IMPLICATIONS OF WEATHER MODIFICATION

People setting out to change the weather should be prepared to deal with their neighbors and, possibly, the courts. If one farmer seeds clouds and more rain falls on his land, did he cause it to fall, and did he "steal" the rain that might have fallen downwnd? If another farmer seeds approaching clouds in an attempt to reduce hail damage, will she at the same time reduce the fall of rain? If a hail-suppression project is commissioned by fruit and vegetable growers, how will cattle ranchers react if rainfall is below normal?

Questions such as these have raised tempers, led to lawsuits, and stimulated legislation that has virtually banned cloud seeding in Pennsylvania. In most cases, the courts have been confronted with insurmountable difficulties in discriminating facts from opinions. Until more is known about the effects of cloud seeding on rain, hail, and other weather elements, it will be difficult to adjudicate questions of the ownership of rainwater and damages following cloud-seeding activities.

According to federal law, individuals engaged in weather-modification programs must provide the National Oceanic and Atmospheric Administration with information such as when and where they seeded and the objective of the operation (that is, to dissipate fog, to increase rain, to decrease hail, or otherwise). More than 30 states have laws that in one way or another exert some control over weather-modification activities. Most scientists and engineers involved in these problems believe that until more is known, it is premature to establish federal regulations calling for the licensing of cloud seeders and the issuance of permits for seeding operations.

Some cloud seeders and other weather modifiers make fantastic claims about their capabilities for increasing rain or snow. A common gimmick is to flash newspaper clippings or even quotations from the Congressional Record. These are not reliable guides to a person's integrity or ability to change the weather. Such information can be obtained from the American Meteorological Society, in Boston, or the Weather Modification Association, in Fresno, California.

CHAPTER 8
Energy Supplies and Consumption

Most of the energy used to move people and machines, to heat and cool buildings, and to power commerce and industry comes from oil, gas, and coal; wood-burning, hydroelectric, and nuclear power plants supply small but important fractions of the total energy requirements of the world. Other sources, such as solar energy, geothermal energy, and windmills, contribute less than one percent to the total energy consumption.

Most experts anticipate that in future decades, supplies of crude oil and gas will diminish appreciably and become increasingly expensive. By the early part of the next century, coal and nuclear power are expected to be the major fuels for the production of electric energy. Even with enormously greater investments of tax dollars, solar energy and other sources are not likely to yield more than 10 percent of the needs of the United States by the year 2000.

ENERGY AND THE ENVIRONMENT

In recent years, there has been a dramatic slowdown in the construction of nuclear power plants in the United States. This has come about because of a fear—whether rational or irrational—of radioactivity. Many people worry a great deal about a nuclear catastrophe. Press reports about what might have happened at the Three Mile Island power plant (Figure 8-1) in March 1979 and the movie *The China Syndrome*, which depicts an accident similar to the one that occurred at Three Mile Island, have created deep-seated anxieties. The very real problems of the disposal of nuclear wastes, worries about losses of nuclear material during transport, and the admonitions of celebrities on television talk shows have succeeded in creating a feeling of potential nuclear holocausts in everyone's backyard.

So, then, what about the huge stores of coal buried in various parts of the United States? The chief reasons why so little coal is used today stem mostly from environmental considerations. When coal is burned, fly ash

Figure 8-1   The Three Mile Island nuclear generating station.
(Courtesy of Metropolitan Edison Co.)

and gases such as sulfur dioxide and carbon dioxide are released. Government air-quality standards require that emissions of sulfur dioxide and smoke particles into the atmosphere be lower than certain prescribed limits. As a result, coal-powered installations must equip smokestacks with precipitators and scrubbers to take out most of the noxious gases and particles. These steps increase the operational expenses of—and the cost of electricity generated at—such plants.

In assessing the consequences of gaseous and particulate emissions, it is necessary to take into account the atmosphere's capacity for diffusing pollutants. When a high atmospheric pressure center—an anticyclone—and light winds prevail and a low level temperature inversion persists for several days, the pollutants put into the lower atmosphere can accumulate in a shallow layer of air near the ground and pose serious health hazards. It should also be recalled that sulfur dioxide is a major contribution to the acidification of rain (see Chapter 2).

To maintain air quality at levels considered to be acceptable, the federal government adopted regulations governing emissions—particularly of sulfur dioxide and solid particles—into the air. In the 1960s and 1970s, restrictions led many electric power companies to convert from coal to oil and gas, which contain less sulfur and are therefore "cleaner." Following the dramatic rise of crude oil prices by the Organization of Petroleum Exporting Countries (OPEC) in the seventies and several episodes of gasoline and fuel oil shortages in various parts of the United States, however, the federal government instituted programs to encourage energy conservation and the use of fuels other than petroleum.

Electric power companies have been using natural gas and coal to a greater extent than in the past. Conversions from oil-powered generators to those using gas and coal are expected to increase in the future. When sulfur-rich fuels are used, meteorological conditions should be carefully monitored and predicted. When low-level inversions and stability are expected—that is, when air pollution potential is high—smokestack emissions should be reduced.

As noted in chapters 2 and 5, fossil fuels—oil, gas and coal—release carbon dioxide in the atmosphere. The concentration of this nontoxic gas (which has a residence time in the atmosphere of about four years) has been increasing for the last hundred years. It was about 300 parts per million of air in 1890 and, if fossil fuels continue to be the major source of energy around the world, it could be twice that level by the middle of the next century.

Evidence suggests that this trend could lead to global warming and, possibly, disastrous societal consequences. If this hypothesis were validated, public policy would have to be to develop—as quickly as possible and whatever the cost—energy sources that emit little or no carbon dioxide or to find economic ways to reduce carbon dioxide released into the air. In the meantime, public policy is that power companies must meet the day-to-day needs of society.

CLIMATE AND ENERGY NEEDS

A large share of the energy consumed in the United States goes into heating homes, factories, and offices. This means, of course, that peak energy demands occur in the winter. Fuel suppliers have found that energy requirements can be estimated from local averages of annual *heating degree-days*. The number of heating degree-days on any day is the number of degrees by which the average temperature falls below 65°F. During any particular winter, the actual accumulated number of heating degree-days may be higher or lower than the climatic averages. Fuel needs increase as wind speeds increase and as clouds obscure the sun, but the temperature effect is by far the most important consideration in estimating the energy requirements of one building or of an entire city. (For a more complete discussion of heating degree-days, see Chapter 12.)

In climatically warm regions, more electricity is used for cooling than for heating. To design air conditioning systems and estimate the amount and cost of fuels necessary to operate them, engineers use information on normal and predicted *cooling degree-days*. The number of cooling degree-days on any day is the number of degrees by which the average daily temperature exceeds 65°F. (Again, see Chapter 12.) Winds and sunshine augment the effects of high temperature in warming a building; the stronger the winds and the greater the incoming solar radiation, the greater the cooling requirements.

Regardless of the climate, one fact remains constant: The better the insulation of any structure, the less the heat transfer into or out of it and the lower the energy costs for maintaining comfortable indoor temperatures.

WEATHER AND FUELS

The delivery of fuels in a timely and efficient fashion requires planning based on current and expected weather as well as on climatic data.

When servicing a large market where winter temperatures are low and variable (Chicago, for instance), a natural-gas supplier must have a large storage capacity. As the heating season approaches, the tanks and underground reservoirs should contain enough gas to meet immediately anticipated needs. The amounts likely to be used will depend on the number and type of consumers and the climatic features of the region. Records of gas consumed in earlier years obviously are good indicators of normal requirements. Weather forecasts should be employed to estimate future energy demands. Forecasts of temperature, winds, and cloud conditions for up to several days into the future have a reasonably high degree of accuracy and are valuable in predicting fuel consumptions.

Weather outlooks a month in advance, although not greatly reliable, are of value when used in conjunction with climatic averages. If competent meteorologists are predicting below-normal temperatures, suppliers should prepare for an increased demand by increasing quantities of gas in storage. Many power companies retain the services of consulting meteorologists, who understand the nature of the industry and make weather forecasts tailored for it.

Very cold, snowy winters can seriously affect shipments of coal by train or via barges along normally navigable rivers and lakes. During frigid weather, the coal can freeze into large, solid blocks and must be broken up, at substantial cost, before being fed into furnaces (Figure 8-2).

A prudent course of action would be to use climatic data to estimate the likelihood of extreme cold weather and to govern the amount of coal stockpiled on that basis. During the winter of 1976–1977, the Ohio River and its tributaries froze. Coal deliveries to industrial plants were cut off, shut-

Figure 8-2 Coal frozen in shipment during very cold weather must be fragmented before use. (Courtesy of Chessie System.)

ting down many of the plants. Accurate long-range weather forecasts might have led to a greater stockpiling of coal in order to reduce the effects of the bitter cold.

HYDROELECTRIC POWER

In the United States, hydroelectric power plants supply about 54,000 megawatts of electric power. Although this represents only 3 per cent of the total—supplied mostly by fossil fuels—the electricity produced by water-driven turbines is crucially important in the economy of the nation. Hydroelectric power is clean in the sense that it does not emit pollutants into the environment. Also, this source of energy is renewable provided there are adequate volumes of rain and snow to supply the water needed to drive generators at full capacity (Figure 8-3). During periods of drought, supplies of electric power are likely to fall below the needs of a region, as occurred in California following 1976, the third driest year on record and 1977, the driest. The result was greatly diminished water levels in reservoirs and inadequate electric power generation.

Managers of hydroelectric power companies use long-range weather forecasts to estimate if snow packs are likely to be above or below normal.

Figure 8-3 Hoover Dam and its hydroelectric power plant. Behind the dam is Lake Mead, which stores the water from rain and melted snow. (Courtesy of Bureau of Reclamation, DOI.)

Such estimates are of only marginal value and should supplement regular observations of precipitation. Surveys of snow depth over drainage areas yield good estimates of the quantity of water likely to be available in the future (Figure 8-4).

In the western United States, various power companies, among them Pacific Gas and Electric and the Southern California Edison Company, have for many years retained the services of cloud seeders for the purpose of increasing snowfalls. The evidence of success is subject to considerable debate by the scientific community, but the clients appear to be convinced that the seeders have been doing some good.

Figure 8-4 Snow packs supply water for hydroelectric power. (Courtesy of Bureau of Reclamation, DOI.)

ELECTRIC POWER DISTRIBUTION

The distribution of electric power is subject to several meteorological hazards. The most common, lightning, causes countless outages every year when there are direct hits on power lines or transformers or when lightning induces current surges in the lines (Figure 8-5). Electricity flows from generating stations via high-voltage transmission lines that feed into lower-voltage distribution systems supplying cities, towns, and rural areas. In the United States, the transmission lines are mounted on high towers and attempts are made to protect them from lightning by running grounded wires above those carrying the power. Large circuit breakers are employed to prevent the burnout of transformers and smaller lines in those instances where lightning succeeds in striking the transmission lines. The smaller cables carrying electricity to homes, offices, and factories are equiped with circuit breakers and lightning arresters. The latter are supposed to be activated by rapid voltage increases and current surges.

Notwithstanding the protective schemes, breakdowns continue to occur.

108

Figure 8-5 Electric power lines threatened by lightning. (Photo by Noel M. Klein; courtesy of NOAA.)

There is little that can be done when a lightning stroke makes a direct hit on a transformer, fuses wires, and perhaps sets the transformer afire. A more serious problem that has come to light in recent years (from the research of E. P. Krider, at the University of Arizona, and his associates), is that the buildup of current in a lightning stroke is much faster than the rate assumed to occur in the design of the protective devices in widespread use. This may account for the fact that, too often, circuit breakers and arresters fail, and as a result the voltage and current surges lead to breakdowns in power distribution systems.

In rural areas with older equipment, it is normal for thunderstorms and lightning to frequently cause power interruptions. Strong winds from thunderstorms often cause more trouble than does lightning, especially in places where tall trees grow next to power lines: The winds break off limbs or knock down trees, which fall on the cables and tear them down. The costs and inconvenience of power failures can be reduced by employing modern techniques for detecting thunderstorms and cloud-to-ground lightning over the power line grids. Such information allows the early deployment of repair crews to locations where breakdowns are apt to occur.

Probability forecasts of thunderstorms are particularly useful. Since such predictions give a measure of how widespread the storms are expected to be during a specified time period, they can be used in deciding how large the standby repair crews should be. If the probability of thunderstorms is only 10 percent, a small crew should be able to handle any emergencies. On the other hand, a probability forecast of 60 percent would call for a large number of linemen to be distributed throughout the area, anticipating lightning burning out transformers or winds tearing down wires. Of course, predictions of thunderstorm occurrence sometimes are far off the mark. But in theory, probability forecasts, used quantitatively in planning and scheduling crew sizes, can lead to more efficient maintenance operations.

The effects of freezing rain can be beautiful when seen on a sunny morning following a storm. Power lines and telephone lines coated with glittering ice resemble ribbons of crystals draped over the arms of leaning power poles. (See Figure 4-12.) Unfortunately, the beauty of the view is usually marred by the absence of electrical power and all the consequent problems. In areas where freezing rain is likely to occur, consideration should be given to the use of systems that can withstand heavy ice loads. In some cases, underground cabling, which would be impervious to freezing rain as well as to other threatening weather events, might be suitable.

Meteorologists working for electric power companies give particular attention to winter cyclones likely to produce freezing rain. Sometimes a small change of storm track can mean that, instead of harmless snow or rain, there will be destructive freezing rain. In the one instance, repair crews would have little to do; in the other, full crews would need to be ready to restore interrupted electrical service.

SOLAR ENERGY AND WIND ENERGY

Although solar energy and wind energy contribute very small fractions to the sum total of the energy needs around the world, in some circumstances they are cost-effective. This is usually the case in places far from sources of fossil fuels or electric generating stations.

The amount of solar radiation at any location on the earth depends on the latitude, the season of the year, and cloudiness. The feasibility of a solar energy system at a particular place depends not only on annual insolation but also on month-to-month statistics. Even arid southern Arizona has a winter rainy season, with cyclonic storms that may obscure the sun for many days in succession. In order to cope with periods of cloudy days, a building heated by solar energy requires a standby heat source that uses

Figure 8-6   A large wind driven machine that can produce 2.5 million watts of electrical power. It is one of three in the United States' first large experimental windfarm that was established in 1981 at Goodnoe Hills, Washington. (Courtesy of NASA, photo for DOE.)

conventional fuels. Its type and size depends on estimated energy needs for the occasional cloudy days and the longer episodes where the weather deviates from normal and is excessively cloudy.

Windmills have been used for a long time to pump water and, in more recent decades, to generate electricity (Figure 8-6). Unfortunately, except for some mountaintops, there are few locations where wind speeds are strong and steady enough to produce electric power at costs competitive with other sources. Furthermore, heavy icing of windmills at high elevations too often cause serious problems.

A major disadvantage of wind systems is that wind speeds vary a great deal, and, therefore, the production of electricity bears little relationship, in time, to the demand. There still are no adequate techniques for storing large quantities of electricity that might be generated by strong winds at night when power requirements are low. Wind-powered systems have been most useful in isolated localities having small electrical requirements. In such circumstances, batteries can serve as electrical reservoirs that store energy and smooth out the peaks and valleys in power production.

CHAPTER 9
Agriculture

Good soil, high-quality seeds, and modern techniques for planting, cultivating, and harvesting are essential if farming is to be efficient and profitable. But if the weather fails to cooperate at every stage of the process, yields will be far from optimum. In extreme meteorological circumstances, entire crops can be wiped out. Droughts over the grain belts of the world can lead to widespread starvation. Floods, plant diseases, and insect infestation can have similar consequences.

To maximize food production, the best agricultural practices available, an understanding of the relevant climatological factors, and a knowledge of past, present, and expected weather are essential. In some circumstances, it is necessary to change the growing environment to withstand the threats of killing frosts, destructive winds, or inadequate precipitation.

Most of the processes involved in the growing of vegetation or in the raising of domestic animals are temperature dependent. Equally important are adequate supplies of fresh water, delivered on schedules determined by the plants or animals.

Most of the world's grain comes from dry farming, that is, from agriculture that relies on rain falling directly on the plants. In arid areas, farming requires irrigation, a practice being used to an increasing extent over the grain belts. Unfortunately, in many areas—for example, the Great Plains and the southwestern deserts of the United States—the rate at which irrigation water is pumped out of underground aquifers (water bearing layers of permeable rock, sand and gravel) far exceeds the recharge by precipitation. As a consequence, water tables have been dropping steadily and pumping costs have been rising. The future of irrigated agriculture in such regions is bleak unless new sources of water are found.

Humidity plays an important role on the farm because it influences the water needs of vegetation. Some plant and pest diseases are humidity dependent. Certain animals thrive better at low relative humidity, particularly when temperatures are high.

Wind and hail can have devastating effects on agriculture. As noted in Chapter 3, violent thunderstorms and hailstorms moving across the grain-fields of the United States, Canada, and other countries cause tremendous damage every year (see Figure 3-16). Fruit orchards and vegetable farms in many parts of the world are similarly afflicted.

Someday, perhaps not too far into the future, it may be possible to predict accurately the onset of such severe storms and to reduce their severity by means of cloud seeding or some other weather-modification procedure. Using cloud seeding for suppressing hail or for increasing rain-fall during dry periods is a chancy practice, however, while the use of climatological information and weather forecasts involves few risks and offers great rewards.

TEMPERATURE

In order for a plant to grow to fruitful maturity, the period between the last killing frost in the spring and the first killing frost in the autumn must be long enough for the particular plant species to go through its life cycle. For convenience, this *growing season* is sometimes defined as the number of consecutive days in which the air temperature is continuously above 32°F. Since different kinds of vegetation respond differently to tempera-ture, growing season requirements vary from one crop to the next. It also varies according to latitude, altitude, and proximity to large bodies of water. For example, on the basis of some 40 years of records, the growing season is considered to be about 120 days in the Great Plains along the Canada–United States border. In central Texas and Oklahoma it is about 220 days; in central Florida, about 320 days.

The actual growing season as defined by the period between killing frosts in spring and autumn can be somewhat longer or shorter than the one defined by the 32°F threshold. Some plants are sturdier than others and can survive temperatures in the 20's. An important factor that should be recognized is that the temperature of the leaves can be significantly different from the minimum temperature for the day measured in a stan-dard instrument shelter. The National Weather Service mounts its ther-mometers about five feet above the ground. At night, particularly when the air is dry and the sky is clear, the leaves radiate directly into the night sky and, by so doing, lose heat faster than does the air above them. As a result, leaf temperature can be substantially lower than air temperature. In these circumstances, some crops will suffer frost damage even when the official minimum temperature is above 32°F. In assessing the likelihood of frost damage, it is important to know where the temperature measure-ments are made. Temperatures can vary appreciably from place to place.

Figure 9-1 Orchard heaters used to combat frost in citrus orchard in Florida. (Courtesy of R. C. J. Koo, University of Florida, Gainesville.)

As noted in Chapter 5, in hilly and mountainous regions, radiation effects coupled with cold-air drainage govern local variations of temperature. Cold, heavy air collects in the valley bottoms under a temperature inversion. In such a circumstance, air and plant temperature are higher on the hillsides than they are in the lower elevations (see Figure 5-3). In the arid parts of Arizona and California, frost-sensitive vegetation, such as citrus, is more likely to thrive in the warmer thermal belts than in the colder lower terrain.

When frost threatens vegetation, it sometimes is possible to modify the growing environment by means of orchard heaters (Figure 9-1), power-driven propellers that push warm air down, or flooding of low-lying plants. These schemes can be effective as long as temperatures are not too low and winds are light. The value of these procedures also depends on the type of vegetation and the stage of growth. With most frost-sensitive vegetation, when temperatures are in the low 20's and the winds are moderate to strong, substantial crop losses are inevitable.

For any particular crop to be grown successfully, not only does the growing season have to be long enough, but there also must be adequate heat available. This is often measured in terms of *growing degree-days* (GDD),

Table 9-1   The Zero Temperatures of Various Crops

Crop	Zero temperature (°F)
Peas	40
Oats	43
Potatoes	45
Sweet corn	50

Source: H. J. Critchfield, *General Climatology,* Prentice-Hall, 1974.

which is similar in concept to the heating and cooling degree-days discussed in Chapters 8 and 12.

The number of growing degree-days for any type of vegetation on any day is the difference between the average temperature on that day and the so-called zero temperature of the crop (Table 9-1). For example, on a day in which the average temperature is 72°F, the number of growing degree-days for sweet corn, which has a zero temperature of 50°F, is 22, that is, 72 minus 50.

Starting from the day of planting, the number of degree-days is accumulated day by day. For each crop there is a minimum total number of degree-days necessary to allow it to pass successfully from planting to harvesting. Obviously, regions with high summer temperatures will have more accumulated growing degree-days than will regions with cooler temperatures. St. Louis, Missouri, would register many more than San Francisco, even though the latter city's growing season is longer.

In order to use a single map for all crops, the *Weekly Weather and Crop Bulletin** computes daily growing degree-days above a base of 50°F and limits maximum daily temperature to 86°F and minimum daily temperature to 50°F. (For crops having a zero temperature below 50°F, adjustments can be made to these figures. For example, for peas with a zero temperature of 40°F, more traditional total GDD can be estimated by adding 10 GDD for every day in the summation period.) Starting on the first of March, the growing degree-days are totaled daily and published once each week. The bulletin dated September 3, 1980, included the map shown in Figure 9-2.

If the climatic data show that, in any region, the available number of degree-days is fewer than necessary for any particular crop, the crop should

*Published by the NOAA/USDA Joint Agricultural Weather Facility, USDA South Building, Room 3526, Washington, D.C. 20250.

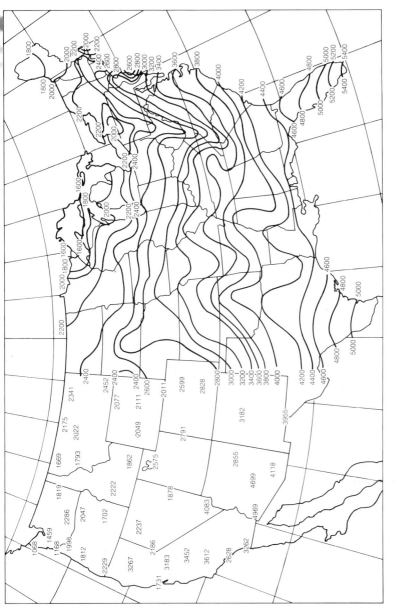

Figure 9-2 Total growing degree-days, March 1 to August 31, 1980. Computed to 50°F base with daily maximum temperature limited to 86°F or less and daily minimum to 50°F or more. (From *Weekly Weather and Crop Bulletin*, vol. 36, September 3, 1980.)

not be planted. In low-latitude areas having long, hot summers, the number of degree-days available may allow two or, in extreme cases, three crops to be planted on the same land during a calendar year.

The yields of crops depends on other temperature-related factors as well. For example, for plants such as tomatoes and potatoes, the cycles of daily temperatures are important. Yields are larger when there are relatively cool temperatures at night (50°F to 60°F) but warm temperatures during the daytime. Sugar beets achieve optimum yields when air temperatures are above 68°F while the plant is growing but are below that when the sugar is being produced in the beets.

The number of hours of sunshine, as measured by the length of the daytime period, influences crop yields. In general, crops planted early in the spring take longer to mature than those planted later.

WATER AND VAPOR

Quite clearly, the results of farming depend on adequate and timely supplies of water. The critical factor is not rainfall but soil moisture throughout the life history of the crop involved. As everyone with house plants or a garden knows, the appropriate conditions depend on the plant species, the stage of growth, the properties of the soil, and air temperature and humidity.

Water in the soil feeds and cools growing vegetation as it passes into the plant through the root systems. The flow of fluid transports nutrients into the stems and leaves. When the air is hot and dry, the stomata of the leaves open and a great deal of water vapor transpires into the air. In the process, the plant is cooled. In a sense, this is the vegetative equivalent to human perspiration.

Because of uncertainties about the quantity and scheduling of watering needed to achieve optimum crop yields, irrigation practices have been less than maximally efficient. Vegetation can survive and even thrive in moderately dry soil, but when there is inadequate water, leaves begin to wilt. A heavy rainfall or deep irrigation will improve the health of the plants, but will not entirely undo the harm caused by the desiccation. This means, of course, that when irrigation is available, a grower should not wait for signs of distress; that is, the plant should not be used as a measure of water insufficiency. The crucial factor, soil moisture, should be monitored directly.

A procedure widely recommended to the home gardener is poking a metal rod or digging a few inches into the soil to see if it is wet. Water should be applied when the soil is dry. Surprisingly, in arid regions, where irrigation is a necessary practice, a great many plants are killed by overwatering. This happens when an amateur farmer, seeing dry surfaces, incorrectly assumes that the dryness extends into the root zone.

Commercial farmers sometimes use soil augers to gage the state of the soil. Another approach is to install electronic moisture sensors whose outputs are recorded continuously. Some authorities believe these procedures are inadequate because they do not measure the wetness at enough points through a deep layer of earth.

An alternative approach to the monitoring of soil moisture is to maintain a water budget of the cultivated field. This involves measuring the water added by precipitation and irrigation and balancing it against the water leaving the field by evaporation and transpiration. This requires computation of the last two processes, which are often lumped together and called evapotranspiration.

It may not be practical for the backyard gardener to do this except in very special circumstances. On the other hand, large-scale commercial growers can afford to set up the bookkeeping system that tracks water gained and water lost. Evapotranspiration can be calculated from formulas developed by agricultural climatologists and a knowledge of existing soil, crop, and atmospheric conditions. This water-budget procedure can be used to maintain soil moisture at desirable levels. When a field is irrigated, this practice also provides for efficient use of water and power.

In nonirrigation farming, success depends on the beneficence of nature in supplying enough rain at the right times. This applies, for the most part, to the grain-growing regions of the world. When droughts occur, the production of wheat, corn, rye, and soybeans is reduced.

As noted in Chapter 4, droughts are natural and inevitable events. Climatic data can be used to calculate the probability of a drought in one region or in several regions at the same time. By means of satellite observations and ground-based data, droughts can be monitored all over the world. Such information can be used to predict food production.

During years when rain is abundant and harvests are bountiful, it should not be forgotten that the meteorological future will not always be bright. Years of rainfall scarcity, dry fields, and parched vegetation must be anticipated, and part of the good harvests must be stored in expectation of poor ones. This practice should be applied nationally and internationally. Otherwise, when nature produces severe droughts in several countries during the same growing season, there could be hunger and starvation on a massive scale, particularly in the underdeveloped countries.

CLOUD SEEDING

If rain is inadequate and crops are wilting, should attempts be made to change the weather? As mentioned in Chapter 7, it still has not been shown convincingly that cloud seeding can increase rainfall by appreciable amounts over the major agricultural regions of the world. Furthermore, there is a possibility that in some meteorological circumstances, cloud seeding might *decrease* rainfall. Nevertheless, the decision on whether or not to seed clouds requires the weighing of possible benefits against possible losses.

Droughts arise from lack of rain-producing clouds. The fundamental cause is found in abnormalities in the general circulation of the atmosphere. Since cloud-seeding procedures cannot possibly succeed unless there are adequate seedable clouds, cloud seeding cannot terminate a drought. On the other hand, if suitable clouds are present, it might be possible to increase rain enough to improve yields by an amount exceeding the costs. In most cloud seeding operations it is virtually impossible, however, to ascertain the effects of cloud seeding, since what would have happened naturally cannot be known. Of course, if abundant rains fall and the crops are restored to productive vitality, it may not matter much whether the seeding caused it or it came from heaven.

The cost of cloud seeding per acre is usually small compared with the per-acre value of the crop. Nevertheless, if no rain is produced, even low costs are too high. Claims of cloud seeding causing drought-breaking rainfalls should be treated with skepticism. Operational cloud seeding represents a gamble whose outcome will be difficult or impossible to determine.

PLANT DISEASES AND PESTS

Weather events can play important roles in the occurrence of disease or pest infestations. Winds carry spores or insects from one field to the next. In many instances, the invasion of diseases or insects depends critically on the temperature and moisture of the air.

Many plant varieties are subject to their own particular afflictions. For example, potatoes are sensitive to a blight that, in serious cases, can cause a great deal of damage and widespread hardship. The mass migration from Ireland to the United States starting about 1850 resulted in part from an extreme case of potato blight. It has been found that potato blight is most likely to occur 7 to 21 days after a period of at least 48 hours during which the air temperature is not less than 50°F and the relative humidity is not below 75 percent. The plants are particularly sensitive to the disease in their early stages of growth, when the shoots are small with respect to the tubers. Fortunately, temperatures during this stage are usually below 50°F in potato-growing regions, and blights do not occur. But when the weather deviates from climatic normals, the results can be devastating.

Many types of diseases that manifest themselves as mildew, rusts, and scabs as well as blights develop and propagate most rapidly in warm, humid weather. The likelihood of disease is an important factor in determining which crops are to be found in particular regions of the world. For example, because of the high risk of rust, little wheat is grown in humid, tropical latitudes, even though there is ample heat and the growing seasons are long.

Cold, dry winters can effectively reduce the incidence of diseases and insects. On the other hand, abnormally warm and humid winters can set the stage for serious infestations during the growing season.

In addition to stimulating disease problems, high temperatures and humidity act to magnify insect populations. Like spores, insects are transported from field to field by winds. Sometimes air turbulence carries insects several thousand feet high, where relatively strong winds transport them great distances.

For many years the standard way to combat plant diseases and insects was to use chemicals. Typically, the home gardener sprinkles or dusts tomatoes, cucumbers, and other popular backyard vegetables with pesticides. The large-scale farmer uses a spray rig attached to a tractor or an airplane (Figure 9-3). It is becoming increasingly clear that, if not properly employed, these techniques can be hazardous because most pesticides and fungicides are potentially toxic to humans.

Figure 9-3   Airplane spraying crops. (Courtesy of the U.S. Department of Agriculture.)

Whenever toxic substances are to be used, certain precautions beyond reading the labels must be taken. First, the user should check the weather forecast. If rain is expected in the near future, use of sprays should be delayed until after the rain. Second, the user should take into account expected atmospheric stability and winds. For maximum effect, it is best to spray late in the day, after cooling has begun. Ideally, the winds should be very light and a temperature inversion should exist to suppress vertical mixing. The effects of winds can be particularly serious when spraying from an airplane. The fine mist containing the chemicals can easily drift over areas populated by people, animals, and vegetation that might be harmed by the spray.

There are times, however, when it is essential to disperse insecticides from the air. Such was the case during the summer of 1981, when the Mediterranean fruit fly invaded California. The only practical means to deal with this major threat to fruit and vegetable production was to use aircraft to spray the infected areas with malathion.

There is a growing interest in reducing the use of chemicals in the war against plant diseases and to employ what are perceived to be less risky alternatives. One approach is to develop plant species that are resistant to the prevalent disease. This procedure can be quite effective when the nature of the seed stock is reasonably well known.

The use of hybrid seeds has stimulated yields per acre, but the cost has sometimes been greater susceptibility to disease. Consider, for example, the case of corn. Through the 1960s, a single hybrid strain represented about 85 percent of the seed used on roughly 60 million acres of farmland. The strain, developed over several decades, inherited its biological characteristics from a single male-sterile plant found in Texas in 1950. Over a long period, it suffered only mild bouts with Race T fungus, so called because of its usually virulent effect on the Texas hybrid. The infections were mild because, over many years, the weather did not favor the spread of the fungus. But in 1970 the unexpected happened.

The spring of that year was unusually wet over the southeastern United States and was accompanied by scattered reports from corn growers in those states of blighted leaves, decaying ears, and rotting stalks. The summer was wet and warm over the Middle West, and spores that had been carried northwest by wind found fertile conditions. By mid August 1970 an epidemic was plaguing the corn fields of Illinois and Indiana. Damage was estimated at $1 billion.

Fortunately for the corn growers and the hungry of the world, 1971 was a cool year and the epidemic was not repeated. In subsequent years a strain of seed resistant to Race T fungus became available. Time will tell if the new hybrid corn is susceptible to some other, as yet undetected, disease.

An interesting approach to the treatment of insect infestation is the use of natural enemies. This technique has been used successfully in California to deal with the walnut aphid. Average annual damage to walnuts exceeded $1 million during the early 1970s. Parasites from France and Iran were introduced to combat the aphids. Within two years of the arrival of the second type of parasite, the aphids were controlled.

WINDS AND SHELTERBELTS

Wind has important effects on agriculture. Excessively strong winds can cause serious physical damage to leaves and branches. They can knock over cultivated crops and even large trees and strip fruit and nuts from branches.

An indirect but important effect of wind is an increase in evaporation and transpiration, especially when the air is hot and dry. Without adequate soil moisture, vegetation can be overstressed and yields of food and fiber can be reduced.

In areas where frost represents a potential hazard—such as the citrus growing regions in the southwestern United States—the winds can be either helpful or harmful, depending on the cause of the low surface temperatures. When the frost results from radiative cooling to the night sky, moderate and strong winds can stir the air and prevent the formation of a temperature inversion (see Figure 5-3). On the other hand, when air temperatures are subfreezing through the lowest layers of the atmosphere, winds aggravate the frost problem.

In regions where strong winds are common during the growing season, farmers often use shelterbelts—rows of trees, bushes, or fences oriented perpendicular to the prevailing wind direction. Designed to break the wind and reduce its speed over cultivated areas, such windbreaks diminish damage to vegetation and loss of water through evapotranspiration. In snowy regions, shelterbelts, by reducing wind speeds, increase the amount of snow that accumulates over adjacent fields, thus increasing soil moisture.

FORESTS

The forests of the world represent a renewable resource of great value. Their productivity depends on adequate precipitation, heat, and sunshine. Like their agricultural counterparts in the open fields, woodland plants are subject to a wide variety of diseases and insects that are weather and climate dependent. In addition, the forests are particularly susceptible to

124

Figure 9-4 Lightning is a serious threat to forests. (Photo by David Baumhefner, courtesy of NCAR/NSF.)

damage by fires. Many are started by people, but lightning is the most common igniter (Figure 9-4). On the average, more than 9,000 fires are started by lightning every year in America's forests and grasslands. They destroy timber, wildlife, watersheds, and recreational facilities.

Forest fire potential increases as fuel moisture—the water content of the living trees, bushes, and grasses and of the dead material lying on the forest floor—decreases. Dried-out limbs, leaves, and the remains of cutting operations can be particularly flammable after long periods of hot, rainless weather.

During droughts, fire danger is high in forests and grasslands even in climatically wet areas. In the more arid regions of the world, such as the southwestern parts of the United States, forest fire risks occur almost every year. Arizona and neighboring areas usually get little precipitation in May and June, months during which temperatures can exceed 100°F at lower elevations. Forest fire dangers in June and early July, before the start of the summer rains, can be very high.

In California forests, brush and grass fires are most common during the dry months from May to September. The burns are particularly serious after wet winters that stimulate native vegetation to grow luxuriantly. During the hot, dry months of late spring and early summer, the green matter dies and dries. It represents a plentiful supply of fuel for fires started by lightning or people. During such periods, campers, picnickers, and smokers must be very careful. Once started, a fire can spread rapidly, particularly if winds are brisk (Figure 9-5).

In many places the potential for fires is reduced by thunderstorms, the very events that are likely to ignite the forest fires. It is fairly common over the entire Rocky Mountain region for spring thunderstorms to find dry forests. The storms commonly have high cloud bases and yield relatively little rain. As a consequence, the lightning they throw out ignites the dry timber, but the rains they produce are not enough to prevent the spread of the blazes. Forest fires can get out of control fairly quickly, especially on dry, windy days.

Figure 9-5   Forest fire. (Courtesy of the U.S. Department of Agriculture.)

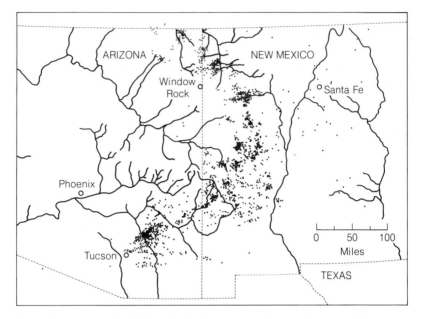

Figure 9-6   A map of 2,229 lightning flashes observed over a 1-hour-and-49-minute period on July 1, 1979, by stations at Tucson, Phoenix, Window Rock, and Sante Fe. (From E. P. Krider *et al., Bulletin of the American Meteorological Society,* September 1980.)

In recent years new techniques have been developed for identifying and locating lightning strokes most likely to initiate fires; lightning of relatively long duration is particularly dangerous. The Bureau of Land Management and the U.S. Forest Service have begun using a network of instruments developed by E. Philip Krider, of the University of Arizona, and Martin A. Uman, of the University of Florida, to map lightning over millions of acres of forests in the western states, including Alaska (Figure 9-6). Early detection of areas under heavy lightning attack should make it possible to anticipate fires and mount effective countermeasures quickly.

WEATHER INFORMATION

In order to optimize agricultural production and protect forests and grasslands from fire damage, it is essential for appropriate weather information to get to agriculturalists quickly. This seldom happens, partly because so many agencies are in the act. Weather forecasts are generated by the National Weather Service; climatic data is collected and distributed by the National Climatic Center and by state climatologists and state universities; farmers get much of their information from agricultural experiment stations and cooperative extension services associated with colleges of agriculture at nearby state universities. The pipelines of data, weather forecasts, and advisories related to such items as planting, spraying, irrigation, and harvesting sometimes become clogged and slow flowing.

Farmers and foresters whose operations are too small to hire their own consulting meteorologists must depend mostly on radio and television for information, which usually falls far short of that needed to make their operations most effective. In 1979 and 1980, scientists at the University of Wisconsin-Madison and at the University of Kentucky, in cooperation with the National Weather Service and the U.S. Department of Agriculture, experimented with television as a means of disseminating weather and climate information. The Green Thumb Project enabled farmers to use simple television devices to request, via telephone lines, a wide variety of data, forecasts, and advisories. These programs required the close cooperation of meteorologists, agricultural experts, and people skilled in communication techniques. Until such a system, based mainly on existing technology, is operational, it will be necessary to use currently available resources. If you need agricultural weather information, start with the land grant college in your state and the National Weather Service. Find out what services are available and use them. Subscribe to the *Weekly Weather and Crop Bulletin*, cited earlier in this chapter. If you run a large agribusiness, an agricultural meteorologist on your payroll would be an asset.

CHAPTER 10

Transportation and Travel

The effects of the atmosphere on airplanes have been evident since the Wright brothers made their first flight. As a result, an appreciable share of the meteorological activities around the world has been devoted to serving the needs of aviation. In the United States, federal legislation requires the National Weather Service and the Federal Aviation Administration to supply weather services to the airline industry. Private pilots usually can get assistance from government weather offices.

In contrast, people who travel the highways of America get relatively little specialized weather service. It is true, of course, that motor vehicle operations are only infrequently subject to weather-induced delays, dangers, and inconveniences. But many drivers starting a cross-country trip do not give much thought to weather conditions likely to be encountered along the route and, even if they did, would not know how to get appropriate information and advice beyond tuning in to local radio reports.

The operators of boats and ships suffer almost as much meteorological uncertainty as do land-based travelers. Mariners have access to general forecasts of wind and wave conditions but, unlike airline pilots, usually do not get up-to-the-minute advisories.

In order to minimize the weather hazards involved in transportation and travel and, where possible, reduce the costs, it is necessary to know the nature of the hazards.

WEATHER ON THE HIGHWAYS

Governmental officials who plan highways should be aware of the role that weather plays in the flow and safety of motor vehicle traffic. They should consult records of the frequency and severity of fog, snow, blowing snow or sand, strong crosswinds, and flooding to select routes over which the likelihood of closure will be small and the hazards few. Sound planning in the early stages will pay dividends later in terms of reduced accident rates and increased traffic capacity.

For a motorist, the first rule in avoiding weather hazards and delays is to listen to the local weather experts. They are not always right, as everyone knows, but they have a fairly good batting average. If the forecast calls for hazardous conditions, the motorist may decide to delay a trip until the weather improves. Before beginning a long drive into unfamiliar territory, a driver should check the terrain, the climate, and the chances of rain and snow along the route. In winter, mountain passes may be closed by snow, and driving over ice-covered sloping roads is dangerous.

Fog is a nuisance that calls for lower speeds and cautious driving. Because fogs occur when humid air is cooled, they are denser and occur more frequently during the cooler parts of the day and night. (See Chapter 4.) Therefore, as a general rule, trips through foggy regions should be planned for the warmer, sunlit part of the day.

Along certain coastal areas, at regular intervals, fogs move in from the sea during the evening and night. Such is the case along the coast of California in the summer, when warm, humid air blows inland over the cold waters of the current flowing southward just offshore (Figure 10-1). Some very dense, widespread, long-lasting fogs occur under warm fronts

Figure 10-1 A low fog partly obscures the Golden Gate Bridge in San Francisco, California. (Courtesy of L. Blodget, San Francisco Convention and Visitors Bureau.)

Figure 10-2   St. Louis, Missouri, on January 31, 1982, following 13.9 inches of snow. (Photo by W. E. Kesler, courtesy of *St. Louis Post-Dispatch*.)

when falling rain evaporates and supplies enough water vapor to the air to cause condensation.

On clear nights in the early autumn, when the air is moist, nocturnal radiation often leads to fogs over the eastern United States. In the West, these fogs occur most often in autumn and winter. The coolest air drains into low areas—river and valley bottoms—where fogs first appear, initially in patches and then in a spreading layer of ground fog. In such places, drivers should be aware that small, scattered patches of fog may indicate widespread fog ahead.

The best way to deal with fog is to stay informed by listening to up-to-date weather reports and forecasts and to drive defensively.

Snow is another major weather hazard. In addition to making roads slippery, a foot or more of snow can virtually immobilize a major city. On rural highways, plows and blowers can move the snow off the roads and onto open fields. But where do you put snow in the canyons of New York, Chicago, or St. Louis (Figure 10-2)? In warmer climates where snow is infrequent and people are unaccustomed to icy streets, even a few inches of snow leads to many accidents and traffic jams.

If a snowstorm occurs at night, the mayor of a city can declare a state of emergency; residents can stay at home while attempts are made to clear the streets and sprinkle them with salt and sand. But when heavy snow falls during normal working hours, commuters may find the streets impassable. The usual result is abandoned, snow-covered vehicles that make it doubly difficult to open up the roadways. When heavy snows are imminent, it may be best to close the schools and public offices, advise the citizens to stay off the streets, and order the city's snow-clearing equipment into readiness.

Ice is another serious road hazard—and not only in winter. In spring and summer, hailstorms occasionally lay down enough ice to cause problems. But in winter freezing rain, in particular, can turn a highway into a skating rink (Figure 10-3). In the United States, freezing rain occurs most commonly in the northeastern states, which are frequented by cold, cyclonic storms. (See Chapter 4.) Driving in freezing rain is not recommended— even walking can be treacherous.

Still another serious road hazard is blowing snow or sand, which can seriously limit visibility. In desert areas, strong winds pick up sand and soil particles and create dust storms that make it hard to see. The winds can also "sand blast" the paint off motor vehicles and pit the glass of

Figure 10-3   Freezing rain causes treacherous layers of ice that contribute to motor vehicle accidents. (Courtesy of NOAA.)

Figure 10-4 Trains can usually plow their way through snow, but they are occasionally stopped by heavy snowfalls. (Courtesy of Chessie System.)

windows and windshields. High-profile vans and trucks can be blown off the road by strong crosswinds. When winds are abnormally strong or visibility is low, it is advisable to look for a place to spend the night.

People whose business involves frequent travel, particularly operators of fleets of trucks, should make a practice of obtaining weather information affecting highway travel and have someone who can interpret it correctly. One possibility is to retain the services of industrial meteorologists to plan routes as aviation meteorologists do for airlines.

Railroads suffer much less from the weather than do cars or trucks. Trains usually can move through wind, rain, and snow although often with caution and loss of speed. Large snow accumulations or avalanches can bring trains to a halt (Figure 10-4), and heavy rains occasionally cause tracks to flood or wash out. But for the most part railroads are unaffected by meteorological events.

BOATING AND SHIPPING

The importance of the weather over open water depends to a large degree on the type of sea craft—a sailboat goes nowhere when the wind ceases to blow (Figure 10-5). In the days of cross-oceanic sailing ships, a captain had to know the climates of the shipping lanes and how to read the sky and the sea. Fortunately, powered ships do not have to worry about light

Figure 10-5 U.S. Coast Guard *Eagle* under full sail. (Courtesy of the U.S. Coast Guard.)

winds. But they do have to be concerned about strong winds, rough seas, heavy fog, and sea ice.

Winds are important for several reasons. A ship can move faster and consume less fuel with a tail wind than with a head wind; on a transoceanic trip, the savings in time and money can be substantial. Circumnavigation of regions of strong winds and high waves may lengthen the trip, but there

Figure 10-6 Ship in a rough sea. (Courtesy of the U.S. Coast Guard.)

will be less risk to the passengers and cargo. There is also the added benefit of greater comfort, particularly for those who suffer from seasickness.

An ocean voyage from New York to England is likely to be more pleasant than the reverse trip. Eastbound, a vessel usually sails with the wind. With a westerly wind of 20 knots,* a passenger on the deck of a ship moving eastward at 15 knots experiences a refreshing 5-knot breeze. On a westward passage, however, there would be a 35-knot gale blowing over the ship.

Over the northern Atlantic in winter and the tropical Atlantic from July to October, cyclones represent serious threats to shipping. The cyclones of the north are cold, sometimes yielding enough snow to coat a vessel with ice. The winds may be 50 knots or more—not enough to damage or sink a large ship, but enough to stir up the sea to an impressive degree (Figure 10-6). Many passengers on expensive luxury liners (and many more

*1 knot equals 1 nautical mile per hour equals 1.15 statute miles per hour. 20 knots equals 23 miles per hour.

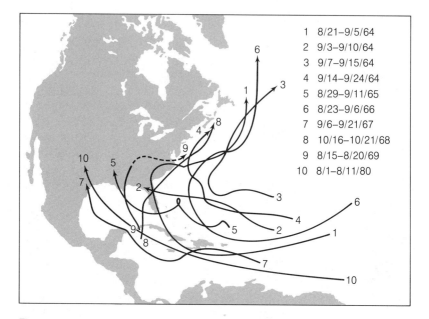

1	8/21–9/5/64
2	9/3–9/10/64
3	9/7–9/15/64
4	9/14–9/24/64
5	8/29–9/11/65
6	8/23–9/6/66
7	9/6–9/21/67
8	10/16–10/21/68
9	8/15–8/20/69
10	8/1–8/11/80

Figure 10-7 Tracks of selected Atlantic hurricanes. (U.S. Government weather map.)

World War II sailors in Liberty Ships) have suffered apparently endless days of agony as they sailed across the violent North Atlantic.

Hurricanes are the real monsters of the sea. Those that menace the United States develop in the trade wind belt over the tropical seas of the North Atlantic. (See Chapter 3.) Hurricanes normally follow a path west through the trade wind region; as they approach North America, they curve north, then northeast (Figure 10-7). Sometimes a storm follows an erratic course that is difficult to predict. When hurricanes move over land or cold northerly waters, they are separated from their main energy source, warm ocean water; the winds diminish and the storms weaken.

Wind speeds in hurricanes are sometimes greater than 150 miles per hour, in a circular vortex more than 50 miles in diameter. Over the open ocean, the winds in an Atlantic hurricane can create waves 35 feet high. When waves generated in different parts of the storm cross one another, the resulting peaks can be mountainous. A Japanese naval vessel that inadvertently sailed into a typhoon in 1935 reported 60- to 100-foot waves.

Satellites track hurricanes and similar storms all over the world from their early beginnings to the final stages of dissipation (Figure 3-13). Satellites observe the clouds in a hurricane, but cannot satisfactorily measure the maximum wind speeds. When a storm is within a few hundred miles of land, specially instrumented airplanes and radar are used to observe its position and strength (Figure 10-8). By monitoring radio reports, a ship's master can stay informed about the location of tropical cyclones and be in a position to circumnavigate them.

Some cyclonic storms along coastal areas or at sea are not adequately observed or predicted, especially in winter. The consequences can be disastrous. For example, on November 22, 1980, an unexpected violent storm hit the rich fishing grounds at Georges Bank about 120 miles off Nantucket. Winds of 80 miles per hour and 50-foot waves sunk four boats and badly damaged four others. Four crewman lost their lives in the incident.

Adequately measuring the state of the atmosphere over the vast ocean expanses is a great challenge. Such elements as wind, temperature, cloudiness, precipitation, and sea state are observed directly in very few places. Measurements come mostly from island bases and from military and commercial ships, a limited number of instrumented buoys, and airplanes. Weather satellites can measure some of these properties some of the time, but they do not observe ocean currents, wave conditions, and water temperatures when clouds are present, nor do they yield sufficiently accurate

Figure 10-8 Hurricane Donna observed on a radar set at Miami, Florida, on September 10, 1960. The distance scale is given by the circle shown to be 100 nautical miles from Miami. (Photo by L. F. Conover, courtesy of the U.S. Weather Bureau.)

measurements of maximum wind speeds. The space technology for making such observations exists, but the funds for designing, launching, and managing an ocean satellite system have not been available.

Another hazard to ships is sea ice. Icebergs have been of particular concern in the North Atlantic, especially since the allegedly unsinkable *Titanic,* on its maiden voyage from England to New York in April 1912, collided with an iceberg and sank to the bottom. Most icebergs in the Atlantic Ocean are large blocks of ice that have broken off from glaciers along the western coast of Greenland and the east coast of Ellesmere Island. After falling into the sea, the icebergs are carried south in the Labrador Current, just off the east coast of Canada. Some of them are then picked up by the North Atlantic Current and float east toward Europe.

Typically, Atlantic icebergs are hundreds of feet long. The largest recorded iceberg in the Arctic was about 1,500 feet long. In the Antarctic, huge pieces of ice break off the ice shelves that extend from the continent into the oceans (Figure 10-9). These icebergs can be more than 50 miles long and 20 miles wide.

Figure 10-9   U.S. naval vessels clearing an iceberg from the channel leading to McMurdo Station in Antarctica. (Photo by A. W. Thomas, courtesy of the Naval Photographic Center.)

Figure 10-10   The U.S.S. *Edisto* breaking through sea ice in the Greenland Sea. (Courtesy of the Naval Photographic Center.)

Ice floats because it is less dense than water, but only about one-seventh of its volume is above sea level. When you see the tip of an iceberg towering 100 feet above the water, you can be sure that there is a lot more of it hidden from view.

The Arctic regions are covered with layers of ice that change with the season and with the climate. The perennial polar ice cap extends south and covers about three-quarters of the Arctic Ocean. Ice thickness averages about 10 feet, but there are ridges that are very much thicker. In the summer, there is some melting and a reduction in the mass of the ice cap.

Beyond the polar ice is a layer of pack ice (Figure 10-10). A fairly thin layer, 3 to 6 feet in winter, it is most responsive to changes in temperature and tends to melt and break up in summer. During climatically cold periods, such as the early part of this century, the pack ice becomes relatively thick and widespread.

In recent years, weather satellites have been used to map the boundaries of sea ice. This information is made available to mariners who operate in polar regions, where shipping to northern ports in Canada, Greenland, Alaska, and Scandinavia may be curtailed during particularly frigid winters.

The U.S. Coast Guard is charged with tracking icebergs and issuing notices about their locations. A vessel equipped with radar and manned by an alert crew should be safe from collisions with icebergs day or night, under clear or foggy skies. Shipborne radar also serves the purpose of detecting other ships hidden in dense fog. The horns and radios can only warn of the presence of other vessels in the vicinity, but radar can show their positions. Since radar is in widespread use on large ships, it would seem that collisions should not occur. But, as with all other vehicles, ships are run by people, and people do make mistakes.

When routing ocean vessels, ship operators would be wise to get the advice of meteorologists who know how weather affects the marine industry. They can keep track of the changing weather, the state of the sea and ice conditions, and, when necessary, transmit appropriate information to the captains of ships already underway. Such procedures should help maximize operating efficiencies.

AVIATION

Anyone who flies an airplane, a glider, or a balloon should take the weather into account before leaving the ground. Commercial and military pilots have ready access to the necessary information. Airplanes are designed to withstand the normal stresses imposed by violet weather events of the kind discussed in this chapter. Unfortunately there still are those rare circumstances where inclement weather, combined with pilot errors, leads to fatal accidents. The more a flier knows, through study and experience, the smaller the likelihood of such an episode.

The major meteorological factors that affect an airplane in flight are wind, turbulence, lightning, hail, and aircraft icing (that is, the accumulation of ice on the leading edges of an airplane flying through a supercooled cloud). But weather considerations must begin at the runway.

The length of runway needed for takeoff depends on the type and weight of the airplane, the elevation of the airport, the wind velocity, the air temperature, and the humidity. The lift imparted to an airplane's wings at any speed depends on the air density—that is, the mass of air in unit volume of space—which decreases with height. Departing airplanes must move faster in Denver (elevation about 5,300 feet) than in Chicago (elevation about 670 feet) to take off. To reach the higher speed, airplanes in Denver need longer runways. In addition, as the air temperature and (to a lesser extent) the humidity rise, the air density decreases; so longer takeoff runs are needed in summer than in winter.

The altitude of an aircraft is usually measured by a pressure altimeter, which is calibrated according to the average pressure–height relationship of the atmosphere. (See Figure 3-3.) Although labeled in units of altitude, the instrument actually responds to air pressure, which is a function of height. Since vertical distributions of temperature and density vary with time and place, so do the pressure at the ground and the rate at which pressure decreases with height. To take the deviations from average into account, a pilot adjusts the altimeter before takeoff and landing. Knowing the atmospheric pressure at the airport, the pilot sets the altimeter so that it reads the field elevation (above sea level) when the airplane is on the ground. Up-to-date "altimeter settings" are normally supplied, via radio, from airport control towers.

When air temperatures at flight altitudes are lower than the averages used to calibrate the altimeter, the actual altitude of the airplane is less than the one given by the altimeter; air temperatures above the averages have the opposite effect. Knowing the temperature, a pilot can easily compute a corrected altitude.

Two important concerns in air travel are *ceiling*, which is defined as the height of the base of the lowest layer of clouds or other obscuring phenomenon that hides more than half the sky, and *visibility*, the greatest distance at which one can see and identify prominent objects. Low ceilings and visibilities most often result from fogs or stratus clouds, but heavy snow or rain, blowing sand, or dense smoke and haze can also be causes. These conditions are most significant during landings and takeoffs.

In very dense fogs, ceilings and visibilities can be nearly zero, bringing traffic to a halt. Fortunately, these "zero-zero" conditions are not common. More often, ceilings are reduced to a few hundred feet and visibilities to less than a mile, in which cases air traffic continues, though at a slower rate, in and out of airports having suitable radio or radar systems that can guide an airplane to a safe touchdown.

Some types of fogs and low cloud layers form or become more dense on clear nights as a result of cooling by thermal radiation to the night sky. For this reason, ceilings and visibilities may drop during the night and early morning. Pilots of small airplanes, who are often required to fly with the ground in sight, should schedule flights out of fog-prone airports for periods after the sun has burned off the fog and before fog begins to form in the evening or night.

In the widespread cyclonic storms so common in the winter over the middle latitudes, low clouds and precipitation can seriously degrade flight conditions for days on end. A major snowstorm in Chicago can shut down its airports by lowering the ceiling and visibility below permissible flight levels and then burying the runways in snow. Summer rainstorms also can restrict air traffic, but usually for only short periods. Strong shifting winds and downdrafts under a thunderstorm can pose very serious hazards, however.

When aircraft movements in and out of an airport are restricted by fog, it sometimes is possible to ameliorate the situation. As explained in Chapter 7, when fog is supercooled, that is, when it is composed of water droplets at temperatures below freezing, it is often possible to cause the fog to

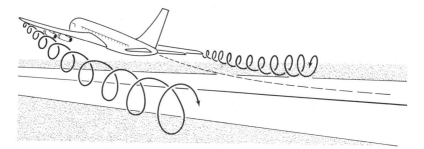

Figure 10-11   Wing-tip vortices produced by an airplane can cause hazardous turbulence for aircraft behind it.

dissipate. Seeding the fog with dry ice or another ice-producing substance converts the supercooled liquid droplets to growing ice crystals. As they fall to the ground, the ceiling and visibility improve.

Since the 1960s, ice-nuclei seeding has been used in the United States, the Soviet Union, and western Europe to clear supercooled fogs over airports. Dense supercooled fogs are not frequent events, but when they do occur they can be costly.

About 95 percent of the fogs over airports in the United States are warm fogs, that is, they have temperatures above freezing. Ice-nuclei seeding will not clear them. Over the last few decades, tests have been run on the effectiveness of the hot blast of jet engines to dissipate warm fogs. (See Chapter 7.) Research is continuing in the United States, but no airports are as yet equipped to dissipate such fogs on an operational basis.

Atmospheric turbulence is another problem in air travel. Most turbulence merely causes annoyance to flight crews and discomfort to passengers. Occasionally it can be severe enough to injure people not properly strapped in their seats or to cause structural damage to an aircraft.

Turbulence occurs when wind velocities vary greatly over short distances. If this occurs, the air breaks down into eddies resembling the whirls seen around rocks and other obstacles in a fast rushing river. Airplanes themselves, particularly the large widebody jets, cause a stream of turbulence in their wakes. As the airplane moves through the air, vortices of air are created at the end of each wing (Figure 10-11). Eddies break off and travel along the ground or through the air with the wind, constituting a hazard to airplanes that take off, land, or fly close behind large ones. An airplane flying through a region of eddies is subjected to rapid accelerations that buffet the airplane up and down and from side to side.

The degree of turbulence depends on the size and weight of the airplane as well as on its altitude and airspeed—the slower the plane, the less severe the effect. The result is analogous to the one experienced when driving an automobile over railroad tracks—the lower the speed, the less the turbulence experienced by the car and its passengers. When flying through turbulent air, it is essential to follow the aircraft manufacturer's instructions on safe airspeeds.

Atmospheric turbulence usually can be attributed to three main causes: convective currents that result as warm air rises and cool air sinks, as in thunderstorms; vertical motions induced by obstructions such as hills and mountains; and strong wind shear, that is, large variations of wind velocity over small distances.

Turbulence caused by convection occurs when the air temperature is highest at the earth's surface and decreases with height. Such conditions commonly exist on summer days but also occur in winter, when, for example, cold air from Canada moves over warmer surfaces such as the Great Lakes. Over hot desert regions, low level convection currents, sometimes called *thermals*, are particularly noticeable. An airplane near the ground is subjected to almost continuous low-intensity turbulence. Although it exists throughout the layer of convective air motions, which may extend to a height of several thousand feet in winter and to more than ten thousand feet in summer, this type of clear air, low altitude turbulence is usually only an annoyance that represents no danger to flight safety.

When the atmosphere is sufficiently moist and unstable, convective currents can be strong and extend to great heights. Cumuliform clouds may form and grow to become massive thunderstorms. (See Chapter 3.) Within them, there are updrafts and downdrafts whose speeds may exceed 60 miles per hour (Figure 10-12). These drafts in themselves do not constitute turbulence—they can carry an airplane up or down several thousand

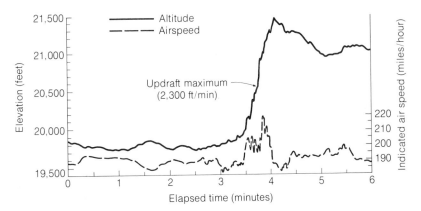

Figure 10-12   Altitude and actual airspeed of a P-61 airplane flying through a thunderstorm. The plane experienced severe turbulence when it flew into the strongest part of the updraft at the 3.5-minute mark. (From H. R. Byers, *Bulletin of the American Meteorological Society*, May 1952.)

feet, but, at least in theory, the altitude change can occur fairly smoothly within the drafts. At the boundaries of the drafts, however, where the vertical air velocities change greatly over small distances, eddies are produced that can cause severe turbulence.

Strong downdrafts under thunderstorms are particularly hazardous. T. T. Fujita, of the University of Chicago, calls them "downbursts" and has shown that they have caused a number of crashes of commercial airliners. Fujita defines a downburst as an event where the downdraft speed at a height of 300 feet becomes comparable to or greater than the approximate rate of descent or climb of a jet airplane on a final approach or takeoff. The downward-rushing air strikes the ground and spreads outward as a high-speed, turbulent wind.

In an active thunderstorm, a pilot also has to contend with heavy rain, lightning and occasional hail. Since the early 1950s, commercial airliners have been equipped with weather-avoidance radar. In addition, the Federal Aviation Administration has developed a network of ground-based radars that maps thunderstorms and makes it possible to direct airplanes around them. Unfortunately, flights through thunderstorms still occur in takeoff and landing and continue to present serious flight hazards (Figure 10-13).

At 4:05 P.M. on June 24, 1975, Eastern Airlines flight 66, a Boeing 727, ran into heavy thunderstorm rain at a height of 500 feet on its final approach

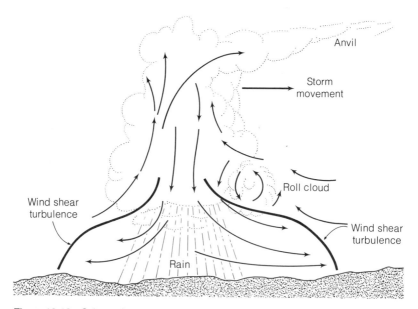

Figure 10-13   Schematic representation of winds and turbulence under a thunderstorm. (From *Aviation Weather*, U.S. Government Printing Office, 1975.)

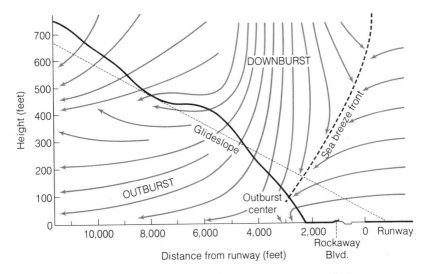

Figure 10-14 Path (solid line) of Eastern Airlines flight 66 when it crashed on June 24, 1975. Also shown is the glideslope (dotted line) the airplane should have followed for a safe landing. The vertical scale is exaggerated with respect to the horizontal scale by a rate of 10.1. (From T. T. Fujita and F. Carcena, *Bulletin of the American Meteorological Society,* November 1977.)

into John F. Kennedy International Airport in New York (Figure 10-14). As the plane flew into the downburst air at 400 feet, its flight speed dropped from 138 knots to 122 knots in 7 seconds. At 200 feet, the airplane encountered a 22-feet-per-second downdraft that carried it to the ground short of the runway. The crash killed 113 people.

There have been a number of other crashes attributed to downburst effects. A Continental Airlines flight crashed on takeoff from Stapleton Airport in Denver on August 7, 1975. An Allegheny Airlines flight on its final approach into Philadelphia International Airport on June 23, 1976, crashed after flying through the outrushing air of a downburst. On July 9, 1982, notwithstanding control tower warnings of the possible existence of strong thunderstorm-caused wind shears, a Pan-American 727 crashed shortly after taking off from New Orleans International Airport. The death toll was 153, 145 of whom were aboard the airplane. This tragic accident has made air traffic controllers and pilots even more aware of the dangers of intense thunderstorms.

When the wind is strong, an obstruction as small as an aircraft hangar creates eddies that can subject an airplane to turbulent motions. When approaching or leaving an airport in strong, gusty winds, it is essential that an airplane's speed be great enough to prevent a stall or loss of control.

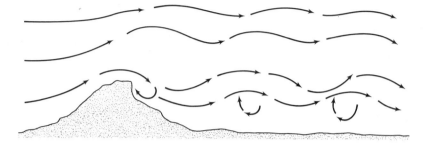

Figure 10-15 Typical configurations of airflow when strong winds blow across a mountain range. Dangerous downdrafts may be encountered on the lee side of a ridge, and the series of waves and rolling vortices can cause severe turbulence.

Turbulence induced by hills and mountains is a form of clear air turbulence, commonly called CAT. The turbulence resulting from strong winds blowing over mountains can be severe and extend through a great depth of the atmosphere. Under certain conditions, air currents develop a strong wave action on the lee side of a mountain range (Figure 10-15). Immediately downwind of a ridge, the air sinks, beginning a giant roll that continues with strong rising currents further downwind.

The updrafts in mountain waves may extend to altitudes of over 30,000 feet. Gliders have gone even higher as they soared in the waves downwind of the Sierra Nevada in California. In some cases, turbulence associated with updrafts can be severe enough to structurally damage an aircraft. A pilot flying into the wind toward a mountain must be aware of the possible presence of a strong downdraft, which can carry the airplane into the ground.

Often a train of mountain waves is virtually cloudfree and extends more than 100 miles downwind of the ridge. But, as noted in Chapter 4, when there is adequate moisture in the air, clouds form in the updraft portions of the wave pattern. In some cases the clouds appear to be nearly stationary and remain for hours; time-lapse photography shows that the wave clouds actually are steadily forming in the rising air and evaporating in the sinking air.

Pilots operating over mountainous terrain should remember that when winds exceed about 25 knots at summit levels, turbulence is likely. Stronger winds and the presence of mountain-wave clouds indicate that the chances of encountering turbulence are appreciable. A pilot who is weather-wise will recognize conditions where turbulence may exist and avoid them if possible. The best course of action is always to check with the nearest weather office, which will have wind, cloud, and other data as well as reports of other pilots who have flown through the region.

Another important class of clear air turbulence is that produced when winds are strong and wind shear is high. In some circumstances, in a layer of the atmosphere with high wind shear, the air moves in the form of waves, much like ocean waves approaching a beach (Figure 10-16). The waves grow in amplitude and roll and break as the air becomes a turbulent mixture of eddies of many sizes. The conditions favorable for this sequence of events often are found in association with the jet stream. (See Chapter 5.)

By flying in the jet stream, airplanes can take advantage of tailwinds that reduce flight time and fuel consumption. For example, an airplane traveling at an airspeed of 550 miles per hour with a tailwind of 100 miles per hour would have a groundspeed of 650 miles per hour. The extra 100 miles per hour could shave nearly an hour off a trip from Los Angeles to New York.

One of the chief tasks of aviation meteorologists is to plan routings that reduce flight times while keeping turbulence to an acceptable level. For many years, scientists and engineers have been trying to develop an effective technique for detecting clear air turbulence ahead of the airplane so that the pilot has a warning of its existence and can take action to avoid it.

Figure 10-16   Wave cloud over the foothills of the Rocky Mountains. The cloud dissipated after about 15 minutes. (Photo by Charles Semmer, courtesy of NCAR/NSF.)

The consequences of clear air turbulence can be very serious: On April 3, 1981, a United Airlines DC-10 flying over Missouri encountered severe clear air turbulence. The airplane reportedly lost about 2,000 feet of altitude and was shaken violently. Passengers who were not strapped in were thrown around the cabin, some hitting the ceiling. Fourteen were injured; seven required hospitalization. The DC-10 itself suffered no damage, and the passengers who had their belts on survived the incident with no more than frightening stories to tell. The possibility of suddenly encountering clear air turbulence is a good reason for always keeping your seat belt buckled when flying, whether or not the seat belt light is on.

Fortunately, layers of clear air turbulence are usually fairly shallow—a few thousand feet thick—and an airplane can get out of the strong turbulence by changing altitude. Sometimes a flight track just a few miles further from the jet stream core leads to smoother air.

A proven airborne instrument for detecting clear air turbulence does not exist, but Peter M. Kuhn, during his tenure at the Environmental Research Laboratories in Boulder, Colorado, developed a device that may do the job. It is an infrared radiometer that senses water vapor inhomogenieties associated with the breaking waves in a wind shear layer. In 1981, Kuhn was granted a patent, entitled "Device for detecting clear air turbulence by remote sensing."

According to Kuhn, the device should be capable of giving a pilot three to four minutes warning of the existence of clear air turbulence. A large avionics company, in association with a major airline, is attempting to develop Kuhn's CAT detector for commercial use. If the device lives up to expectations, it will be a major step toward improving the safety and comfort of jet travel.

The threat of lightning is a frightening thought to airline passengers who have not flown a great deal. Fortunately, the dangers to commercial and military airplanes are small. A lightning strike might burn a few holes perhaps a few tenths of an inch in diameter near the ends of the wings, or damage electronic communication and navigation equipment, without jeopardizing the safety of the flight. Before techniques were developed to protect airplanes, some planes were severely damaged by electric arcs that started fires or that caused explosions when lightning ignited the vapors in their fuel tanks. The chance of such happenings today is minimal, although a nonmetallic airplane or one whose various parts are not properly bonded electrically could be in serious trouble if hit by lightning. Fliers of such aircraft should stay on the ground when thunderstorms are likely to occur.

One of the hazards of a lightning strike, particularly at night, is that the bright flash can temporarily blind a pilot. A long-standing procedure has been to turn up the cockpit lights and put on sunglasses, which reduces the period of blindness.

Figure 10-17   Hail damage to the leading surfaces of an airplane. (Courtesy of NCAR/ NSF.)

Hail is a problem for airplanes wherever large thunderstorms occur, but the highest frequency of hail is on the Great Plains. (See Chapter 3.) An airplane encountering hailstones having diameters exceeding about half an inch can be badly damaged (Figure 10-17). Hailstones usually are found inside thunderstorms; therefore, an airplane can avoid hail by staying in clear air outside the clouds. Sometimes, however, hailstones fall out of the side of a tilted cumulonimbus cloud. In some hail shafts, the stones are so far apart as to be invisible to the naked eye at a distance of some miles. Airborne radar can detect hailstones and makes it possible for a pilot to circumnavigate the hazardous region. The safest procedure, particularly in areas where hail is common, is to stay at least five miles away from thunderstorms and not to fly under cumulonimbus anvils.

The problems of aircraft icing are mostly encountered by airplanes that fly below about 25,000 feet. At higher elevations, the clouds are composed mostly of ice crystals that do not stick to an airplane. On flights through supercooled clouds and freezing rain, ice can build up on propellers and the leading surfaces of an airplane (Figure 10-18). Sufficiently heavy ice accumulations cause increases in the weight and drag of the airplane. Decreases in thrust and lift tend to cause decreases in airspeed and losses in altitude. Icing can also impair the engine performance of some aircraft. In rare—but potentially disastrous—circumstances, the ice can extend back over the wings or tail section and cover the flaps and other control surfaces.

A flight through a growing cumuliform cloud at altitudes where temperatures are between about 32°F and 5°F commonly leads to aircraft icing. But airplanes usually pass through such clouds in a few minutes and only thin layers of ice form. Serious icing problems can arise when an airplane

Figure 10-18   Heavy icing on the forward tip of the wing of a King Air airplane. (Courtesy of Wayne R. Sand, University of Wyoming.)

flies through a supercooled cloud for a long time. Pilots should be aware of the dangers of icing and check the likelihood of its occurrence with aviation meteorologists.

During a heavy snowstorm, particularly when temperatures are not too low and the snow is wet, an airplane can accumulate large quantities of ice on its wings and other surfaces. If not removed before takeoff, the ice can change the flight characteristics of an airplane and constitute a serious hazard. On January 13, 1982, an Air Florida jetliner leaving Washington (D.C.) National Airport with a heavy load of snow and ice stalled on takeoff. It crashed into the Fourteenth Street bridge across the Potomac River and sank in the river. Only 5 of the 79 people on board survived; 4 people in automobiles on the bridge died in the crash.

Ice on runways can pose another serious problem for pilots operating in areas that experience snow and freezing rain. On January 23, 1982, a World Airways DC-10 carrying 190 passengers skidded off the end of an ice-coated runway at Logan International Airport in Boston and sank in the shallow water of Boston Harbor. Except for 2 passengers whose lives were presumably lost by drowning, others who were on the airplane escaped with minor or no injuries.

Before taking off, airline pilots are briefed on important weather conditions expected along the route and are kept informed of any changes. Such procedures serve to reduce the hazards and minimize the inconveniences. Even so, weather factors, particularly turbulence in flight, low ceilings and visibilities, and heavy rain or snow at the terminals, sometimes play havoc with aviation schedules. But the occasional discomfort of a rough flight and delays in landing and takeoff are tolerable prices to pay for the speed and convenience of travel, especially since the number of weather-related accidents experienced by commercial carriers is very small. Private pilots should follow the example of their counterparts in the cockpits of the world's airliners and learn how to use weather information effectively.

CHAPTER 11
Comfort and Health

It is easy not to appreciate the full impact of the atmosphere on human well-being—physical and psychological. Violent weather is obviously traumatic, causing injury and death to thousands every year; the effects of polluted air, though not so dramatic can still be tragic, particularly for the very young and very old with already existing lung problems. Sometimes the weather has such subtle influences that the hows and whys remain a mystery. For example, certain asthmatics find miracles in the desert air of southern Arizona while others find only disappointment, and the reasons for the differences still have not been found.

It is sometimes difficult to specify in detail how the weather affects human behavior and psychological well-being, but there is no doubt that it does. Who can forget the joys of the first warm, sunny days of spring after a seemingly endless cold, gloomy winter? Also, it is well established that the strong, dry, gusty winds of the alpine foehn and the California Santa Ana are associated with increases in abnormal behavior.

No one needs to be told which weather conditions are physically pleasant and which ones cause discomfort. The most important element is temperature, but strong winds make cold days seem colder and hot days hotter and have many other effects as well.

Even at moderate temperatures, atmospheric humidities affect human perception of air temperature. When the relative humidity is low, most people react as if the temperature were below its true value; when humidity is high, the opposite occurs.

Investigations have been made of the losses and gains of heat by the human body as functions of temperature, humidity, and wind speed. Such information is particularly important in the design of clothing for use by people living and working in extreme environments (Figure 11-1). For example, the maintenance crews along the Alaskan oil pipeline must be protected from the frigid conditions that can cause frostbite or hypothermia.

153

Figure 11-1 In regions of very low temperatures, specially designed clothing must be worn to maintain normal body temperature. (Courtesy of the Geophysical Institute, University of Alaska, Fairbanks.)

When temperatures are high, physical activity leads to increases in body temperature and loss of water. Too much of either can cause acute exhaustion or heat stroke. On hot days, manual labor and exercise should be restricted and the intake of water should be increased.

THE WINDS IN WINTER

The wind ventilates the body and can transport heat and water vapor to or from it. On a dry day, the ventilation leads to enhanced evaporation of perspiration, causing a loss of body water and greater cooling. The lower the air temperature, the greater the heat loss. The wind serves to amplify the effects of low temperatures; for this reason, wind effects can be expressed in terms of temperature.

The term *wind chill factor,* or *wind chill index,* represents the cooling effects of specific temperature and wind conditions on a human being. Most body heat is lost through the skin. For this reason, insulation (that is, clothing that has low heat conductivity) can markedly reduce the chilling effects of cold, windy air. On cold, dry days, about one-fifth of the body's heat loss is attributed to breathing. Face masks can reduce this loss, but only by a slight amount.

Equations can be derived for calculating the cooling power of the wind and expressing it in terms of a wind chill temperature. The stronger the wind, the greater the loss of heat and the lower the apparent temperature. The difference between air temperature and wind chill temperature depends on such factors as the size of the individual, the clothing worn, and the physical activity involved. Wind chill temperatures for an average adult who is wearing winter clothing (including gloves) and is walking are shown in Table 11-1. Note that at a wind speed of 5 miles per hour the wind chill

Table 11-1   Wind Chill Temperatures (°F)

Air temperature (°F)	Wind speed (mph)								
	0	5	10	15	20	25	30	35	40
32	34	32	27	24	21	17	14	12	10
28	30	28	23	19	15	12	9	6	4
24	26	24	19	14	10	7	3	0	−3
20	23	20	14	9	5	1	−2	−6	−9
16	19	16	10	5	0	−4	−8	−12	−17
12	15	12	6	0	−5	−10	−15	−19	−24
8	11	8	1	−5	−11	−16	−21	−26	−32
4	7	4	−3	−10	−16	−22	−28	−34	−40
0	3	0	−7	−15	−22	−28	−35	−42	−49
−4	−1	−4	−12	−20	−28	−35	−42	−50	−58
−8	−4	−8	−16	−25	−33	−41	−50	−59	−67
−12	−8	−12	−21	−30	−39	−48	−58	−68	
−16	−12	−16	−26	−36	−45	−55	−66		
−20	−16	−20	−30	−41	−52	−63			
−24	−20	−24	−35	−47	−58				
−28	−24	−28	−39	−52	−65				
−32	−27	−32	−44	−58					
−36	−31	−36	−49	−64					
−40	−35	−40	−54	−69					

Source: R. G. Steadman, "Indices of Windchill of Clothed Persons." *Journal of Applied Meteorology,* vol. 10, August 1971.

temperature is the same as the air temperature. The winter clothing compensates for the heat loss attributed to a 5-mile-per-hour wind.

As the wind speed increases, the wind chill temperature decreases rapidly. For example, when the air is at 12°F and the wind speed is 30 miles per hour, the wind chill temperature is − 15°F. This means that an adult dressed as noted above would feel the same chilling effect as if the air temperature were actually − 15°F and the wind were 5 miles per hour.

Table 11-1 can be used as a general indicator, but appreciable differences in the physiological responses of different individuals are to be expected. For example, a large man would not be chilled as much as a child under the same wind and temperature conditions.

COMFORT INDEX

Some people enjoy the cold, brisk winters of Omaha; others prefer the warm, humid air of Miami or Honolulu; still others opt for the hot, dry air of Tucson. Personal preference depends on a person's physiology, psychological predisposition, and feelings about the climate of his or her childhood. Any scale relating human comfort to atmospheric conditions must therefore have a large statistical component.

How an individual rates the comfort of the atmosphere depends on various weather elements. Certainly temperature and humidity are important. Winds of more than a few miles per hour also become relevant. Smoke or pollen levels have important effects on certain people, primarily those with pulmonary inadequacies. Some people suffering from arthritis may be affected by atmospheric pressure or changes of pressure.

For a typical healthy adult on a day with light winds, it is possible to specify a comfort—or discomfort—index in terms of air temperature and relative humidity. At low temperatures—below about 35°F—the effects of relative humidity are not important; at high temperatures, high humidities make conditions even more uncomfortable. When the air temperature exceeds 100°F, most people feel hot regardless of the humidity. When the relative humidity exceeds 30 percent at that temperature, the atmosphere can be described as oppressive. A temperature of 82°F becomes oppressive at humidities greater than 70 percent.

The effects of humidity on a person's perception of warmth can also be indicated by a graph of apparent temperatures (Figure 11-2). When relative humidities are low, the perceived temperature is less than the actual air temperature. As relative humidities increase, particularly at higher temperatures, the air appears to be warmer than it actually is. For example, when a shaded, ventilated thermometer reads 90°F and the relative humidity is 60 percent, the apparent temperature is a sultry 100°F.

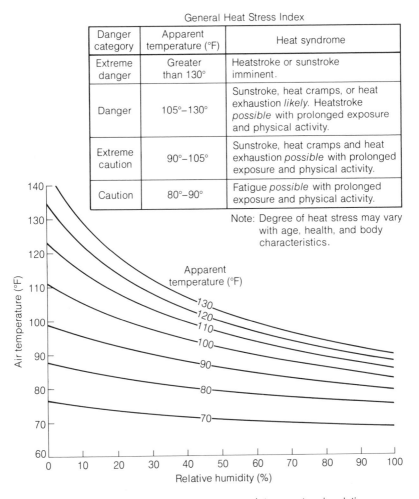

General Heat Stress Index

Danger category	Apparent temperature (°F)	Heat syndrome
Extreme danger	Greater than 130°	Heatstroke or sunstroke imminent.
Danger	105°–130°	Sunstroke, heat cramps, or heat exhaustion *likely.* Heatstroke *possible* with prolonged exposure and physical activity.
Extreme caution	90°–105°	Sunstroke, heat cramps and heat exhaustion *possible* with prolonged exposure and physical activity.
Caution	80°–90°	Fatigue *possible* with prolonged exposure and physical activity.

Note: Degree of heat stress may vary with age, health, and body characteristics.

Figure 11-2 Graph lines indicate apparent air temperature in relation to actual air temperature and relative humidity. The box shows the likely consequences when an adult is exposed to high apparent temperatures [From R. Qualye and F. Doehring (based on calculations by R. G. Steadman), "Heat Stress," *Weatherwise,* vol. 34, pp. 120–124, June 1981, a publication of the Helen Dwight Reid Educational Foundation.]

JOGGING AND RUNNING

It is becoming almost commonplace to see middle-aged joggers dripping with perspiration but determined, notwithstanding the effort and pain, to achieve at least one more mile. Such a sight is a reminder of the fact that the safe limitations of human exertion depend on external as well as internal conditions. On hot, humid days, the normal human body can take less

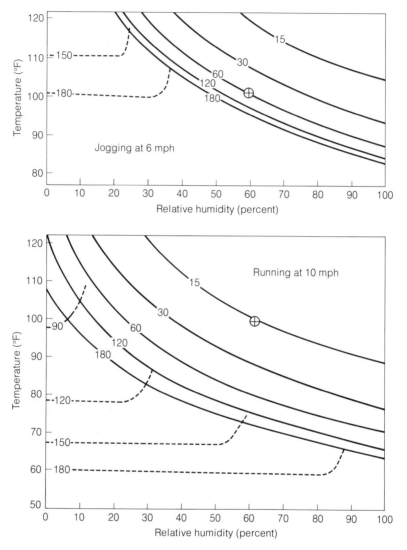

Figure 11-3 Recommended maximum duration of nighttime jogging and running by a lightly clad, healthy adult at various air temperatures and relative humidities. The solid lines show the times, in minutes, required for internal body temperature to reach 104°F. The dashed lines show the times required to lose 5 percent of body weight through perspiration. (From K. C. Young, "The Influence of Environmental Parameters on Heat Stress During Exercise," *Journal of Applied Meteorology*, July 1979.)

punishment than it can on cooler days. Competitive long-distance runners—and those who jog for fun and health, as well—should not underestimate the dangers of heat stress. During the 1973 Boston Marathon, the air temperature was only about 79°F; nevertheless, one runner died and almost a dozen were hospitalized as a result of heat exhaustion during the 26-mile run.

The limits of reasonable exercise have been calculated by Kenneth C. Young, of the University of Arizona, who used a theoretical model of the heat budget of the human body. The analysis took into account—for various levels of exercise conducted over varying periods of time—heat losses resulting from respiration and evaporation, heat gained by direct solar radiation, and heat generated inside the body and transported to the skin.

Young's research yielded graphs showing maximum recommended durations of exercise for various temperature and humidity conditions (Figure 11-3). The durations were established by calculating how long it would take for the internal body temperature to reach 104°F. (Experts have reported that, although some people suffer heat stroke at a temperature of 102°F to 103°F, there is a marked increase of heat disorders when temperatures exceed 104°F.)

Young's graphs show that when the air temperature is 100°F and the relative humidity is 60 percent (indicated by $\oplus$), for example, the maximum recommended duration for jogging at night is one hour, but for running it is about 15 minutes. Obviously, the more strenuous the exertion, the shorter the period over which it should be performed. The upper diagram indicates that on most days (but certainly not all), a healthy jogger should not go on for more than three hours. The combined effects of clothing that retards evaporation of perspiration and solar radiation can increase the effective temperatures by more than 12°F. Runners are advised to wear light-colored, porous clothing and reduce the duration of exercise on hot, sunny days.

Also included on Young's graphs are indications of how long it would take to lose 5 percent of body weight through perspiration. Unless the lost water is replaced, a runner risks dehydration. It is a common practice to spray long-distance runners with water in an effort to reduce perspiration and cool the skin. Young noted that the spraying does some good, but under high temperature and humidity conditions, the benefits are minor.

HIKING AND SKIING

People who find pleasure and peace of mind in climbing over or skiing down mountains have to be aware of the weather factors involved. William E. Reifsnyder, of Yale University, discusses these factors in a book entitled *Weathering the Wilderness*. In addition to describing the climatic characteristics of a number of popular recreation areas, Reifsnyder reviews the potential hazards. Among the most critical hazards are overexertion on hot, humid, sunny days leading to hyperthermia—a dangerous overheating of the body—and more often, a dangerous reduction of body temperature—hypothermia—that can occur when an improperly dressed climber is exposed to low temperature, strong winds, rain, and clouds. On a back-packing trip in high country, warm clothing may be the only means of preserving body heat—and thus life.

Another critically important concern to people who hike and ski in the winter is the threat of heavy, blinding snow and the occurrence of avalanches, large masses of snow that break loose from steep mountain slopes and slide downhill (Figure 11-4). Avalanches can be initiated in a variety of ways. Once they start, they usually do not stop until they reach a flat region in a valley bottom. In some cases the snow can carry along ice, rocks, and soil.

Avalanche dangers are high on steep lee slopes that have recently had more than about two feet of snow. A person traveling in such regions should check with the U.S. Forest Service or National Park Service about the possibility of an avalanche occurring. A sound procedure is to avoid, if at all possible, any valley where there is even a remote chance of an avalanche. If it is absolutely essential to cross a slope heavily laden with

Figure 11-4   An avalanche. (Courtesy of R. L. Armstrong, University of Colorado, Boulder.)

snow, do it in such a way as to minimize the chance of starting an avalanche and maximizing the chance of survival if one occurs. Reifsnyder offers guidelines on how this can be done.

RESORT CLIMATES

For a long time, many Europeans have placed much faith in the curative and restorative powers of clean air, sunshine, and pleasant weather. A 1964 report of the World Meteorological Organization in Geneva used phrases such as "climatic treatment" and "specific climatic therapy." It has been alleged that blood circulation, respiration, and skin condition are made healthier by exposure to favorable weather. These notions have resulted in the establishment of many health resorts in mountainous and southern-coastal areas. Baths in warm, sulfur-laden waters of certain natural springs are often part of the treatment.

The benefit of the redolent waters and the air that surrounds them is debatable, but a week or two in a climatically optimal resort may send a city dweller home with a healthier mind and body. European climatologists have given a great deal of study to the most appropriate attributes of resort areas. To a certain extent, these depend on the purpose of the resort and the conditions of the people it seeks to attract. Generally, anyone seeking a pleasant period of recuperation from an illness is advised to avoid the following conditions: intense heat, particularly if accompanied by high humidity; polluted air, especially if the patient has had some kind of respiratory illness; highly changeable weather with frequent passages of fronts and cyclones; and excessively high elevations, where the presence of oxygen in the atmosphere may be too low.

Sanatoria should be far enough from cities and industries to assure low concentrations of gaseous and particulate pollutants. Local vegetation should be of varieties that produce little pollen. The clean, brisk air often found at moderately high elevations on the lee of a ridge or along a sea coast dominated by light sea breezes is recommended for summer resorts. On mountains or hilly terrain, spas are sometimes located in forest glades, where they are protected from strong winds by tall trees.

Sunshine is considered therapeutic in many parts of the world. The World Meteorological Organization report, cited earlier, discusses the value of solar ultraviolet radiation in "heliotherapy." These rays are "used for their effects on skin cell metabolism, formation of substances such as vitamin D and detoxification processes." Heliotherapy calls for long periods of exposure to the sun. Today, in the United States and a number of other countries, it is recognized that the risk of skin cancer through excessive exposure to sunlight exceeds the benefits of such exposure.

In the Western Hemisphere, there is relatively little stress on health resorts, but a great many people migrate to the sunny southlands in winter.

Most Easterners head for Florida and the islands in the tropical Atlantic, but not in search of cures: The attraction appears to be warmth and sunshine—how good it is to stretch out on the beach with a cold beer while the friends at home are shoveling snow! At the other end of America, in southern Arizona and California, winter finds hordes of so-called snow birds baking in the sun. For some, a trip to the desert falls short of expectation if they do not go home with a dark suntan. Most of these sun worshipers either do not understand the dangers of overexposure to ultraviolet radiation or choose to ignore them. But even a casual observer should recognize that melanoma and the leathery pelts of elderly sun lovers are evidence that too much solar radiation does more harm than good.

HUMAN DISEASES

The relations of certain diseases to the weather are obvious, at least in a general sense. Mortality data show that disease-related deaths are most frequent during winter (Figure 11-5). This is true for most illnesses, but particularly for those involving the lungs. A graph of deaths by all causes in the United States in 1975 displays the same general pattern, but it also shows a pronounced upsurge of deaths in August (Figure 11-6). This upsurge was caused by an unusual heat wave in the heavily populated northeastern states. (A similar episode occurred during the summer of 1980 over the central United States.)

Increased mortality at high temperatures is a consequence of the inability to maintain normal body temperature. The human thermoregulatory system tends to break down as people age. The sweat glands begin to fail, and, as a result, an important cooling mechanism becomes inefficient. In the absence of other means of cooling the body, the stress of high air temperatures can lead to circulatory and other diseases that result in death.

Winter brings increases in the occurrence of colds and influenza; in some years flu reaches epidemic proportions. Occasionally epidemics are predicted by medical experts: In the winter of 1974, the federal government invested millions of dollars in vaccine to combat an expected onslaught of a strain of flu called swine flu. It appears that the prediction of flu epidemics is even more difficult than weather forecasting. The number of cases of swine flu in the winter of 1974 was far less than had been predicted. The experts appear to believe that the vaccination program could have helped to reduce the incidence but probably did not account for the relatively small number of cases.

The precise weather features that favor the occurrence of influenza are not known. Some experts believe that the disease is more likely to develop when relative humidities are below 50 percent and the winds are light. Presumably, low temperatures are favorable for the survival and spread of the virus until it finds fertile resting places in the breathing passages of

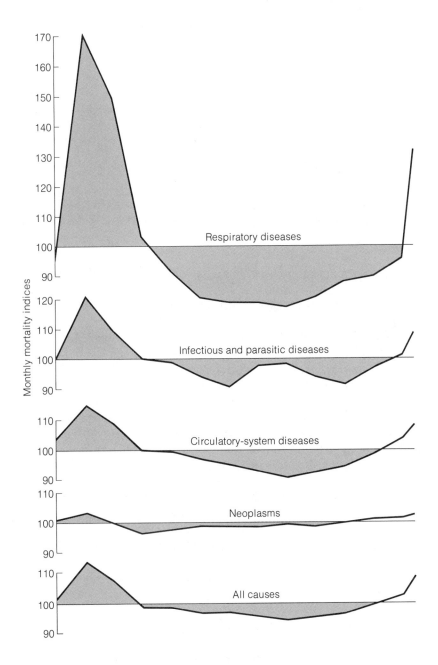

Figure 11-5 Seasonal patterns of disease-related deaths in 1973 in the United States. On each vertical scale, 100 is the 12-month average. (From W. Hodge, "Weather and Mortality," *EDIS,* September 1978.)

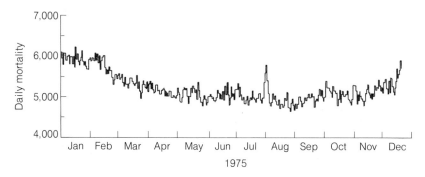

Figure 11-6 Number of deaths from all causes in the United States in 1975. (From W. Hodge, "Weather and Mortality," *EDIS*, September 1978.)

humans, but temperature variations alone cannot explain changes in the frequency of flu from year to year and place to place. It still is not known, for example, whether changes in diets or social habits in winter have any effects of human susceptibility or the spread of flu.

Cold weather also is accompanied by increases in the symptoms of two other common diseases: arthritis and asthma. Hospital admissions for asthmatic patients increase when sudden cold spells occur. These results suggest that asthmatics would be well advised to move to warm, dry places such as the southern parts of Arizona and California. In fact, many who do so experience dramatic freedom from the most prominent asthmatic symptoms, such as recurrent breathlessness. Unfortunately other sufferers find little or no relief. As a matter of fact, some people who arrive in the desert in a healthy state develop respiratory ailments after exposure to the extremely dry air of late spring and early summer.

The relation of asthma to the weather is made even more puzzling by reports from western Europe that the frequency of attacks is low during periods of fog. In southern Arizona, some asthmatics who feel well during the normally dry periods suffer when periods of wet, humid weather occur. How can high humidity be beneficial in one place but harmful in another?

The answer may lie in the complicated nature of asthma. In some patients, the symptoms are triggered by allergies to certain pollens—ragweed, for example—and other airborne pathogens. It seems reasonable to conclude that many victims of the disease have benefited from living in the southwestern deserts because of the relative scarcity of pollen-rich vegetation. But the situation has been changing: Since World War II, there has been a tremendous migration into the Southwest, where the newcomers have transformed desert cities such as Tucson and Phoenix into giant oases. Irrigation, widely used, has greened the cities (Figure 11-7). Trees, bushes, flowers, and grasses that normally could never survive in a harsh arid climate thrive when given adequate water and some fertilizer.

The people have also brought cars and trucks and other sources of smoke and dust. The once crystal-clear air of the desert is less so, especially in the larger cities and in the vicinity of copper smelters and major power plants. The reader should not get the impression, however, that southern Arizona is under a pall of polluted air getting worse day by day. In Tucson, you usually can see for over 40 miles—and on some days more than twice that far. But on most nights, temperature inversions form near the ground and pollens and dusts accumulate to greater extents than in the past. Fortunately, daytime warming serves to mix low-level air through thousands of feet of the atmosphere and disperse the pollutants. Nevertheless, on those occasions when a large high-pressure center stagnates over the region, the emissions of irritants into the air can build up over a period of days and reach levels that cause asthmatics to suffer.

For some types of asthma, relief from symptoms can be found by moving to an area relatively free of those pollens and other atmospheric particles and gases to which a person is sensitive. Differences among patients make

Figure 11-7   Flood irrigation of lawns in Phoenix, Arizona. (Courtesy of Anthony Brazel, Arizona State University, Tempe.)

it virtually impossible to predict the consequences of a move to Arizona, Florida, or any other place, however; the only way to find out is to live in a new location for a period of time. Such an experiment is likely to be expensive, but it might be worth the cost.

Arthritis is the name given to a class of diseases leading to pain and disfigurement of joints. For over two millennia, medical writings have noted the effect of weather on arthritis. Some who suffer from the disease often can predict weather changes with a surprising degree of skill.

Some early European literature noted that arthritics reacted to pronounced cooling and strong winds, but that humidity changes were not particularly important. Complaints increase in autumn and early winter— many arthritics suffer pain and discomfort during periods of cold, humid weather. Because of the highly variable nature of the patients, their medication, and the many interrelated weather events occurring at the same time, it is difficult to interpret these reports.

In the early 1960s, J. L. Hollander and S. J. Yeostros built a controlled climate chamber, at the hospital of the University of Pennsylvania, in which two patients could live comfortably for periods of two to four weeks. The temperature, humidity, and atmospheric pressure could be adjusted without the knowledge of the patients, making it possible to carry out experiments to separate the possible effects of the various weather factors.

In these experiments, arthritis pains increased most often when there was a simultaneous increase of humidity and decrease of atmospheric pressure, a condition which occurs as a front approaches. Successive occurrences of such events seemed to have a "cumulative detrimental effect" on the patients. When humidity and pressure were stabilized, the arthritis symptoms subsided fairly rapidly. These results show that sufferers of the disease should be aware of the approach of fronts, especially rapidly moving cold fronts, because of steep pressure falls and humidity increases that often accompany their approach and passage. If experience verifies the results of the Hollander-Yeostros experiments, medications to deal with pain and discomfort can be programmed accordingly.

As in the case with asthmatics, certain arthritics have found relief in the warm southland. The pain is diminished for many by being able to lie in the sun, but this form of therapy can be overdone. Southerly latitudes offer relief to many arthritis sufferers because major storm tracks are in the middle latitudes. Places such as Florida, Hawaii, Southern California, and Arizona experience fewer frontal passages than do most of the major population centers of the United States and Europe. Therefore, in the more tropical regions, there are fewer cases of the pressure drops and humidity rises that were found to be the triggers of arthritic pains in many of the patients tested by Hollander and Yeostros.

Living is easier in warm climates: Houses tend to be ranch style with fewer stairs to climb; snow and ice do not make walking a dangerous exercise. For a person with painful joints, these factors are important. A move to a warm region where weather changes are relatively few is not likely to cure asthma or arthritis, but it could be beneficial for many sufferers.

HUMAN BEHAVIOR

The psychological effects of the atmosphere are even more difficult to understand than are the physiological ones. As was indicated earlier, the correlation of temperature, pressure, and humidity with certain physical ailments can be examined in controlled laboratory experiments. But the role of the weather in influencing human behavior requires observations of how people respond to preceding or coincident environmental events. Various authors have noted that certain identifiable atmospheric conditions are related to level of mental concentration, desire to work, and emotional well-being. But psychological symptoms vary greatly from one person to the next, and the reasons are far from clear.

It has long been suspected that response to external stimuli (including weather) depends on the physique of the person. On this basis, W. F. Petersen, in his book *Lincoln-Douglas: The Weather as Destiny*, analyzed in detail the effects of weather on the lives of Abraham Lincoln and Stephen Douglas, two figures who dominated the American political scene during the middle of the nineteenth century. Lincoln was tall, thin, introverted, and given to periods of deep depression. Douglas, short, heavy, and extroverted, was not particularly sensitive to the state of his surroundings.

According to Petersen's analysis, Lincoln became physically and psychologically drained during periods of cold, wet weather. He suffered greatly when the woman he loved, Ann Rutledge, died on August 25, 1835, during a period of abnormally low temperatures. Three days later it rained, and Lincoln, already exhausted from hard work and worry, had an emotional collapse.

Six years later, after a stormy relationship with Mary Todd, Lincoln tried to break their engagement. But it was not until January 1, 1841, when a cold front passed and temperatures dropped to $-12°F$, that his level of gloom and despair became extreme and he actually took the drastic step. About two weeks later, another cold front moved through Illinois, and Lincoln's depression was so severe that it was feared he might commit suicide; his friends kept instruments of possible self-destruction out of his sight.

Lincoln's spirit rose when the weather was warm. In the summer of 1862, after months of indecisive action, he went against the advice of his military experts and discharged General McClellan. It was a turning point in the Civil War.

What accounted for the wide swings in Lincoln's emotional state? Were the weather events, especially the sudden temperature drops and the rainstorms associated with cold frontal passages, the causes of his depressions?

If so, how are the associations explained? Is it because of the effects of the physical and electrical states of the atmosphere on the human body—on its temperature, blood pressure, and chemistry? Some students of the subject believe this is the case. They further believe that the results depend on the body size, structure, and composition (that is, fraction of fat, muscle, bone, and so on).

There is no doubt that hot, dry, gusty winds, called *foehns* on the slopes of the Alps and *chinooks* on the eastern slopes of the Rockies, have distinctive psychological and physiological consequences. According to published reports, when foehns are strong, some people find their ability to concentrate decreases, and accidents, crimes, medical complaints, and suicides increase.

Similar symptoms are associated with other strong, dry, gusty winds, such as the sand-filled sharav in Israel. Felix Gad Sulman, who immigrated there in 1932, made extensive studies of the behavior of people before and during the occurrence of the sharav. He concluded that many humans are afflicted with "foehn sickness" and that it commonly begins a day or two before the onset of the winds and continues as they blow. Sulman reported that an abnormal increase of the naturally occurring substance serotonin coincided with the sickness and concluded that that accounted for it. Serotonin, in the central nervous system, plays a role in the transmission of signals among nerve cells. The level of serotonin has been associated with certain mental disorders, such as schizophrenia and depression, but there is still uncertainty about whether the disorders result from too little or too much serotonin. But what specific atmospheric conditions, if any, might affect serotonin or otherwise account for foehn sickness? Sulman proposed variations in the electrical properties of air—in particular, an excess of positive ions—as an answer.

IONS AND ATMOSPHERICS

Atmospheric *ions* are molecules or atoms that have too many or too few negatively charged electrons. For example, when an electron is stripped from a carbon dioxide molecule (CO_2), the result is CO_2^+, that is, an ion with a positive charge. When an electron is added to an oxygen molecule (O_2), the result is O_2^-, a negative ion.

The atmosphere virtually always has a large amount of ions—there are about 16,000 negative ions and 20,000 positive ions per cubic inch of clean outdoor air—but the concentrations are highly variable and depend on the state of the atmosphere. Many studies agree that ions cause changes in bacteria, fungi, some vegetation, and tissue cultures of cells from mammals. But the evidence that the ion properties of air can cause the symptoms of foehn sickness is contradictory.

Sulman concluded that before and during winds such as the foehn and the sharav, there is an increase in the concentration of positive ions that causes a reduction in oxygen consumption by the lungs and the production of excess serotonin. It has not yet been shown, however, that the hot, dry, gusty winds of the world commonly have excessively high concentrations of positive ions. Furthermore, there is no satisfactory explanation of why the symptoms precede, by a day or two, the onset of the winds.

If the cause for foehn sickness (or the many other physical and psychological ailments associated with the weather) is an excess of positive ions, the solution is to increase the concentrations of negative ions in the environment. This can be done in a number of ways, and various types of negative-ion generators are manufactured commercially. Some users are convinced that they are effective and that exposure to high doses of negative ions brings about improved health; others who have tried negative-ion generators have found them to be of little value.

In electrified clouds, particularly thunderstorms, electrical discharges cause radio waves known as *atmospherics*. They account for radio static during periods of active cloud development. In 1963, German scientist R. Reiter reported that on days when there were high frequencies of atmospherics, there were substantially more complaints by "brain patients," "amputation cases," and "chronic patients" and more traffic accidents than on days with low frequencies of atmospherics. It is far from clear, however, whether the atmospherics were the cause of the observed differences in human behavior.

WEATHER–HEALTH DIARY

Any person who suspects that the weather is affecting his or her behavior or physical condition might consider keeping a diary arranged in two columns. For each day, one column would contain a report on the weather, including statistics on temperature, wind, humidity, fog, precipitation, lightning, and thunder; the other column would note emotional and psychological states during the day, such as happiness, elation, tension, irritation, loss of appetite, and similar feelings or responses.

If updated daily for at least a year, such a diary could be used to identify and modify weather-sensitive behavior. If disagreements with family, friends, and associates occurred most often during a particular type of weather, confrontations could be avoided if properly anticipated. If depression and thoughts of suicide were associated with particular weather patterns, moving to a place where the disturbing weather conditions occurred seldom or not at all might allow a person to live a happier life.

CHAPTER 12

Designing Homes and Other Structures

 The chief goals in building a house should be to create a healthy, comfortable, and pleasant environment in which to live and to provide shelter from weather extremes. An essential part of that interior environment is the air, which should be clear of pollutants and have temperatures and relative humidities that satisfy the inhabitants.

In order to achieve and maintain optimum conditions effectively, it is necessary to know the climatic characteristics of the region. Factors such as seasonal variations in the apparent altitude of the sun will influence decisions regarding the type and amount of insulation, the pitch of the roof, the need for and size of air conditioning equipment, and the feasibility of solar energy heating systems. Among the most important climatic elements that must be taken into account by an architect are sunshine, solar radiation, temperature, wind, rain, and snow.

TEMPERATURE

When temperatures are consistently hot, as in tropical areas, or cold, as in polar regions, substantial power plants are needed to either cool or warm the air to make it acceptably comfortable. In desert areas, particularly at low latitudes, the diurnal temperature changes, that is, the differences between daily maximum and minimum temperatures, are relatively large. For example, in Tucson, Arizona, the average daily maximum temperature in June is 99.2°F and the average daily minimum is 64.0°F, a difference of 35.2°F. Outgoing radiation at night causes rapid cooling, and incoming solar radiation through cloudless skies causes rapid warming. Thick walls create thermal lags from day to night that can flatten out the temperature fluctuations. Early settlers in the deserts of the southwestern United States accomplished this by building heavy adobe huts. Bringing cool air into a building at night can reduce its interior temperature to comfortable levels. During the hot daytime hours, the passage of air in and out of the building obviously should be minimized.

171

Winds may either aggravate or ameliorate the effects of temperature. On a winter day in Chicago, for example, the wind, by carrying away heat from a building (or any other body, for that matter), amplifies the effects of low temperature. Table 11-1 shows the effects of wind chill. The stronger the wind on a cold day, the greater the heating requirements to maintain comfortable temperatures inside a building. On hot days, the winds increase the cooling requirements. In windy places, it is especially important to design well-insulated buildings in order to minimize heat transfer through the walls and roof.

On the other hand, when outside air temperatures are moderate, a light wind can be beneficial and can be used to ventilate a building in a desirable fashion. Air blowing gently through a structure will carry away odors and smokes, aid evaporation, and serve to cool the environment and influence

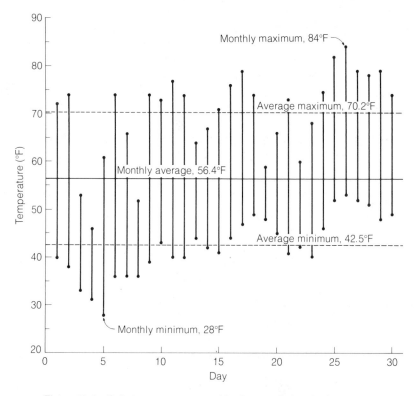

Figure 12-1   Daily temperature record for Denver, Colorado, for April 1981. Also indicated on the chart are the monthly maximum, minimum, and averages. (From *Climatological Data*, vol. 86, April 1981, NOAA, National Climatic Center, Asheville, N.C.)

the temperature of the entire structure. This fact should be taken into account in the design of homes, offices, and factories.

Of particular importance to building design are daily and monthly average temperatures, daily and monthly average high and low temperatures, and daily and monthly temperature extremes. These quantities give a good idea of the types of conditions likely to be encountered in the future.

Climatic archives contain a wide assortment of temperature data and data summaries (Figures 12-1 and 12-2), including statistical summaries

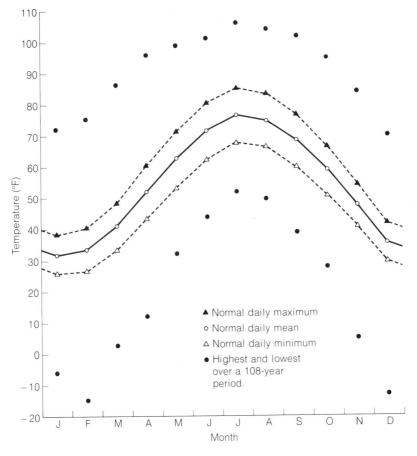

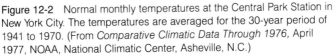

Figure 12-2 Normal monthly temperatures at the Central Park Station in New York City. The temperatures are averaged for the 30-year period of 1941 to 1970. (From *Comparative Climatic Data Through 1976*, April 1977, NOAA, National Climatic Center, Asheville, N.C.)

of heating degree-days, which can be used to estimate the monthly or seasonal heating requirements. As explained in Chapter 8, the number of heating degree-days on any day is the number of degrees by which the average daily temperature falls below a standard temperature—in the United States, 65°F. For example, if the average temperature on a particular day is 42°F, that day has 23 heating degree-days.

The number of heating degree-days is found for weekly, monthly, and annual periods by accumulating the daily values for the days involved (Figure 12-3).

The amount of power needed to cool a building can be estimated from a knowledge of the number of cooling degree-days, the accumulated difference between 65°F and the average daily temperature when the latter is greater than 65°F. Climatic data for the United States show that Miami registers an average of 4,000 cooling degree-days—about four times more than New York (Figure 12-4).

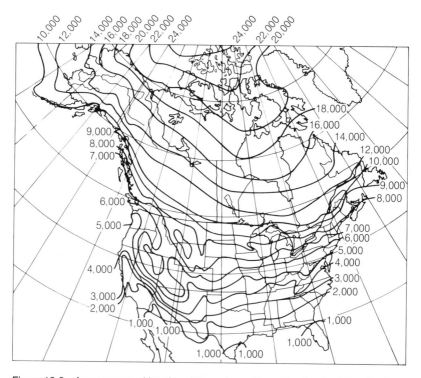

Figure 12-3   Average annual heating degree-days. (From *Handbook of Geophysics*, revised edition, by U.S. Air Force, New York: Macmillan, 1961.)

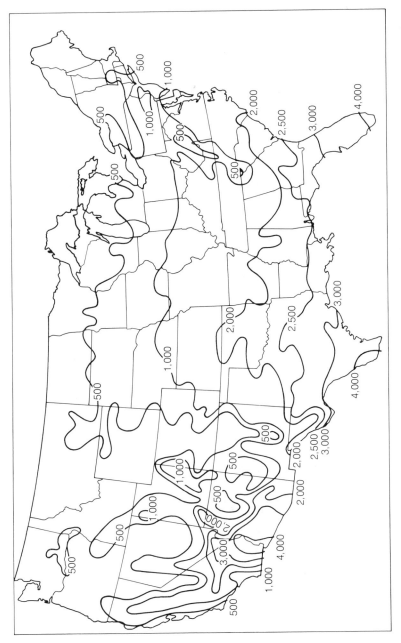

Figure 12-4 Average cooling degree-days, 1941–1970. (From H. E. Warren, S. K. LeDuc, and M. S. Joshua, *Climatic Degree for Energy Demand Assessment*, National Oceanic and Atmospheric Administration, Washington, D.C., November 1980.)

Statistical data on expected weekly heating and cooling degree-days and ranges of possible values for major cities in the United States are prepared and distributed by the Environmental Data and Information Service, a branch of the National Oceanic and Atmospheric Administration. The data are valuable indicators of the relative costs of maintaining a comfortable indoor environment. For example, a building in Chicago would require more than four times the heating capacity of a similar building in New Orleans to maintain the same temperature.

STRONG WINDS

Most of the time, the winds are weak and serve to modify the effects of temperature or humidity. But sometimes the winds can be unpleasant and dangerous; in some instances, winds are strong enough to cause serious property damage and loss of life.

In designing a structure—whether it be a house, school, nuclear power plant, or office building—it is essential to examine the statistical properties of the wind at the building site in regard to the purpose of the structure. Wind statistics should be used to determine the building's orientation with respect to the physical environment. It should be known from which direction strong winds usually come; trees and bushes can be placed to reduce wind speeds.

Often, topography or the orientation of the streets in a large city with tall buildings forms channels for the wind. The Boston area has various examples of buildings that have suffered from such effects. The Green Building at the Massachusetts Institute of Technology, in Cambridge, is located in a place considered a wind tunnel by many people who work there. A large metal sculpture mounted as a windbreak has helped the situation.

The eastern slopes of the Rocky Mountains experience one- to two-day bursts of dangerous downslope winds several times each winter; they occur as a result of rapid downhill flow of air on the lee of mountain ridges. The strong, gusty winds cause havoc with the residents of such Colorado cities as Boulder and Colorado Springs, where they can blow at speeds greater than 60 miles per hour, with gusts exceeding 100 miles per hour in extreme cases.

These winds can damage buildings of all kinds and present problems around entryways. Even such substantial structures as those housing the Air Force Academy, near Colorado Springs, and the National Center for Atmospheric Research buildings, near Boulder, lose some of their easy and pleasant access during periods of strong winds. People approaching these attractively designed entrances are pushed and pulled by the winds, and swinging doors become hazards.

There also are psychological problems associated with certain wind conditions. Some people become depressed, irritated, or frightened during prolonged periods of strong winds. The noises caused by the winds, the creaking of roofs and walls, the threat of blown-in windows, the patter of pebbles and other debris on the roofs and sides of buildings—all contribute to a feeling of anxiety and are a threat to well-being.

A casual examination of climatic records is not enough to identify short-term wind-speed anomalies, particularly in mountainous areas, where they often occur under fair weather conditions. Climatic averages obscure the brief, sporadic high-speed occurrences. It is necessary to search carefully the records of each particular region for such unusual but important wind episodes.

In mountainous terrain, there can be great differences in wind speeds over short distances. For example, on some occasions the winds blow at more than 60 miles per hour at Boulder, Colorado, while at Denver—some 30 miles away—they may be less than 20 miles per hour.

Tornadoes and hurricanes have very high wind speeds. Tornadic winds can exceed 200 miles per hour—powerful enough to destroy mobile homes and small buildings and to do very substantial damage to even the strongest buildings (Figure 12-5). In regions where tornadoes are fairly common (see

Figure 12-5   Tornado damage in Oklahoma. (Photo by Joseph Miller, *The Daily Oklahoman*. Property of Oklahoma Publishing Company.)

Figure 12-6 The effects of storm waves on homes on Fire Island, New York, March 8, 1962. (United Press International photo.)

Figure 3-18), all structures should be designed to withstand the destructive effects of most strong winds. In addition, provision should be made for basements—or public shelters—that can withstand the assaults of severe storms and where residents can find safe refuge when tornadoes are imminent.

Hurricane winds are strongest over the open oceans and maintain high speeds as a storm approaches a coastline. Therfore, buildings along the shores of the Gulf of Mexico and the Atlantic Ocean, vulnerable to approaching hurricanes, must be able to withstand winds that appreciably exceed 100 miles per hour for periods of several hours. A hurricane will also bring heavy rains and crashing waves of ocean water. A structure on a beach will be under attack from water that erodes its foundations and winds that batter it broadside. Flying debris also poses a serious hazard and can do considerable damage.

In addition, hurricanes sometimes spawn tornadoes. A tropical storm sweeping across Florida or Mississippi can have several tornadoes imbedded within it. Any intense cyclonic storm along a coastline can have the same effects as a hurricane (Figure 12-6).

In places for which there are no wind records, an architect, or someone considering building or buying a home in an unfamiliar part of the country, should interview longtime residents, who will know about unusual weather behavior. In an isolated area, it might be necessary to establish a weather station and collect several years of data before engaging in a major building program.

RAIN AND SNOW

Heavy rain and snow can represent serious threats that have to be anticipated in designing or buying a home. Roofs must be designed and built to withstand the expected loads. Snow is particularly troublesome. Even major buildings can cave in when the weight of accumulated snow exceeds the bearing strength of the structure. For example, on January 18, 1978, the roof of the Civic Center Coliseum in Hartford, Connecticut, collapsed under the weight of about a foot of snow. The same storm dumped enough snow on Long Island to cause the dome of the C. W. Post auditorium to cave in (Figure 12-7).

Combining climatic records with a knowledge of meteorological processes makes it possible to estimate likely maximum snowfalls. In regions known to experience heavy snows, such information should be taken into account in the planning of structures.

It seems relatively easy to design a system for effectively draining the rainwater off a roof, but there have been occasions when the accumulation

Figure 12-7 The domed roof of the 3,500-seat auditorium at the C. W. Post Center of Long Island University, in Greenvale, New York, collapsed because of the weight of snow that fell on it in late January 1978. (Photo by Fred R. Conrad/The New York Times.)

of rainwater exceeded the drainage capacity. In such a circumstance, the weight of the water can cause the roof to collapse, as happened at the Kemper Arena in Kansas City, Missouri, on June 4, 1979.

Rain becomes a threat most often because of potential flooding. As land values have increased, there has been greater encroachment into flood plains; structures are being built in places where the chances of major flooding are substantial. Sometimes this is done in ignorance, but sometimes it is a calculated risk by builders who subscribe to the principle of caveat emptor—let the buyer beware.

Federal and local government agencies publish information on the flood potential of rivers and streams in the United States. Wisdom suggests either that building in places of high flood risk should not be engaged in or that the buildings be designed to survive the inevitable floods.

Flood dangers are often expressed in terms of the likelihood of floods of particular severity. For example, the U.S. Geological Survey and the Army Corps of Engineers publish maps and reports showing areas along stream and river channels under the threat of so-called hundred-year floods.

This means that, in a designated area, a flood of the indicated severity would occur, *on the average*, once every hundred years. This does not mean that if there were a flood last year, the next one would not occur for a century: The term *hundred-year flood* means that over a period of 1,000 years there would be about 10 floods; there is no suggestion that they will be equally spaced. In principle, massive floods two years in a row can be followed by several hundred nonflood years. Information on flood risks can be obtained from the Water Resources Research Centers located at all Land Grant Universities or from state water officials.

The likelihood of flash floods is easily overlooked, particularly in arid regions. Often the climatic records are of little help because of the scarcity of weather stations in lightly populated rugged terrain. If an area experiences thunderstorms—even rarely—building should be avoided in canyon bottoms and low-lying land. Not to heed this advice is to invite tragedy: On July 31, 1976, thunderstorms over the drainage area of Big Thompson Canyon in Colorado caused a massive flash flood, washing out houses, roads, and automobiles. The flood left at least 139 dead and caused property damage of nearly $36 million.

Such disasters can be avoided: Flood forecasters in the National Weather Service can estimate the odds of flash floods and can advise land-use planners, developers, home buyers, and campers.

LIGHTNING AND HAIL

By definition, a thunderstorm is a storm that produces thunder and lightning. Therefore, the higher the frequency of thunderstorms, the greater the chance of being hit by lightning.

As the leading end of a lightning channel makes its way toward the ground, it searches for a high point to hit. Tall trees, towers, chimneys, and high buildings are favorite targets, particularly when they are isolated. Such structures can be protected by means of well-designed systems of lightning rods.

Most buildings are immune to hail damage except when hailstones are large; hailstones the size of walnuts can cause severe damage to roofs and windows. In regions where hail is frequent (see Figure 3-18), fragile materials should not be used on roofs. Glass skylights and expansive windows make it possible to appreciate the magnificence of nature, but if they cannot be protected from hail, they might not last long. Thunderstorms producing large hail can also yield heavy rain. If a skylight is shattered, the resulting water damage may be even greater than that caused by the hail.

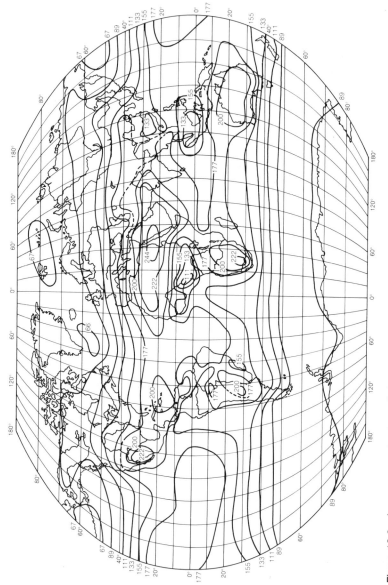

Figure 12-8 Average annual solar radiation, in units of watts per square yard, on a horizontal surface at the ground. (Based on a diagram from W. D. Sellers, *Physical Climatology*, by permission of University of Chicago Press. Copyright © 1965 by University of Chicago Press.)

SOLAR ENERGY AND BUILDING DESIGN

As the costs of fossil fuels increase, alternate energy sources will be developed and exploited. One of them, solar energy, is plentiful and clean; annual solar radiation over the United States ranges from less than 100 watts per square yard to about 230 watts per square yard (Figure 12-8). Therefore, any application involving large amounts of power would have to expose large areas to the sun. Insolation is relatively great over low-latitude arid regions in summer; in cloudy locations and at high latitudes, solar radiation intensity is low. Climatic records contain information on hours of sunshine and energy levels to be expected by the month.

The technology of solar energy utilization, particularly as it applies to individual structures, is getting a great deal of attention. Increasingly, the sun is being used as a source of heat. A well-designed building allows the rays of the sun to bring heat directly into a home, business, or office building (Figure 12-9). Solar application techniques such as this one are described as passive, distinguishing them from active ones whereby solar

Figure 12-9 Passive solar house in Baltimore County, Maryland, designed by Peter Powell. In winter, windows on sloping south-facing wall allow sunshine to warm stone floor of main living area, which is set 4 feet below ground level. In summer, blinds cover the windows, which can be opened to let air in. Windows at the top of the cathedral ceiling provide ventilation. (Photo by Jack Schneider, courtesy DOE.)

Figure 12-10   Solar energy collectors used for heating water for a house in Tucson, Arizona. (Courtesy of Charles Glickman, University of Arizona.)

energy is captured, stored, and redistributed by the circulation of warm air or water.

The orientation of a building and the use of glass and overhangs should be planned with an appreciation of the position of the sun during different seasons of the year. In winter, the sun is low in the sky, and its radiation can provide heat and light if there are adequate window space and few obstructions. Any trees or shrubs on the south side of a building should be decidous and not so dense that they block out the winter sun's rays.

In the summer, particularly in warm areas and southerly latitudes, western exposures should be opaque to the setting sun. During the hottest part of the day, the sun will be high in the sky. Windows should be shaded by overhangs. Vegetation can be used to intercept incoming radiation and add to the beauty of the area.

In many countries, notably Israel and Italy, solar water heaters have been in use for a long time. Only in recent years have they begun to grow in popularity in the United States (Figure 12-10). Large solar energy collectors can supply most of the heat for many buildings or for producing the electricity to drive pumps. For heating applications, heat must be stored in a large volume of water, rocks, or some other substance, and then redistributed efficiently.

Although their initial costs are still high compared with conventional systems that consume fossil fuels, solar energy systems for heating individual buildings or small groups of structures will become more economical as other fuels become more expensive. Energy obtained by solar cells that convert solar radiation directly to electricity are still far too expensive except in very special circumstances: They are cost effective in powering spacecraft and in some very isolated locations far from conventional sources of electricity. One of the goals of solar energy researchers is to develop inexpensive solar cells that can be produced in large quantities. Once that is accomplished, there should be a great expansion in the use of solar energy for many applications.

CHAPTER 13
Music and Art

When the sounds are combined and arranged in succession, the result can be called music. Most music theorists probably would say that unless the tones follow prescribed rules of combination and progression, the result should be described as noise rather than music. Others might take the view that the distinction can only be made by the ears that detect the perturbations of atmospheric pressure that vibrate the eardrums and send sound messages to the brain.

The air is full of sound waves from many sources—automobiles, birds, dogs, children, factory whistles, rustling leaves, and so forth. Someone living in a large city is surrounded by man-made sounds, often too many and too loud. Except in the case of thunder or heavy rain, the sounds of the city drown out "the music of the weather."

W. J. Humphreys, an atmospheric physicist of great renown, uses this phrase as the title of a chapter in his book *Ways of the Weather*. The chapter deals with the origin and propagation of sound waves through the atmosphere. Had the text been addressed to scientists, he might have entitled the chapter "meteorological acoustics."

For the whispering of the wind, akin to the quiet strains of muted violins, to be heard, other sounds must be vanishingly soft. The full range of weather music can be experienced only by a listener in a lonely, wooded countryside. In such an environment, a nearby thunderstorm has the percussive effect of a cannon.

Various sounds of the weather have served as inspiration for many composers. Anyone familiar with the great music of the world knows how the sights and sounds of the heavens have stirred the juices of creation. The weather has inspired other artists—painters, sculptors, dancers—as well as musicians. Before examining examples of the meteorological influences on the fine arts, consider some of the ways that sounds are generated by the atmosphere.

THE MUSIC OF THE WEATHER

When the wind blows through conifers or deciduous trees bared of leaves by winter, the needles and small twigs of the trees are caused to oscillate. A solitary pine, when all other sounds are absent, can produce a solemn dirge as the vibrating needles give off a sighing sound. Changes in the wind modulate the pitch and loudness of the aeolian tones. In a forest denuded of leaves or composed of pines, the somber solos of individual evergreens become a symphony as the sounds from the vibrating twigs and needles combine. The musical murmurs sometimes can be heard more than a mile away from their source.

Wind gusting strongly through a forest on a mountain slope sometimes produces a roaring sound. Again, the sources are the millions of twigs and branches set into vibration. Winds blowing around chimneys and corners of houses produce eddies that give a howling effect, more noticeable inside than outside a house—particularly when a person is alone on a dark night.

Various atmospheric phenomena produce the sounds normally associated with percussion instruments. The most obvious, of course, is thunder erupting with the suddenness of the crash of cymbals. Rain and hail on a roof, particularly a metal one, give the beating of snare drums that builds and falls as the raindrops and hailstones increase and decrease in size and number.

In forests, mysterious sounds sometimes erupt with frightening abruptness. On very cold nights, the water in trees can freeze, causing them to split open explosively with the sharpness of a slaptstick. When the wind is strong, a forest sometimes gives out frightening shrieks: They occur when a tall dead tree falls into the fork of another tree and the wind forces it to slide back and forth like a bow across the strings of a double bass.

People who have heard tornadoes pass over their heads report that the funnels produce their own distinctive roaring sounds. Some witnesses have said that the sound is like the buzzing of millions of bees; others have observed that the funnels give off the noise of freight trains or of nearby jet airplanes

Other weather events could be cited as sources of "music"—for example, the gentle dripping of rain or the sizzle of electrical discharges from pointed objects (known as corona discharges) just before a nearby lightning strike. Clearly, the atmosphere can create its own distinctive acoustical patterns. Composers have heard them and been inspired.

CLASSICAL MUSIC

A. James Wagner, an American meteorologist with a love of classical music, has written about compositions that describe the changes of climate through the year. One of the earliest examples is the well-known eighteenth-century piece *The Four Seasons*, by Italian composer Antonio Vivaldi. In this cycle of violin concertos—created during the middle of the period known as the Little Ice Age (see Chapter 5), when winters were abnormally cold in lowland Italy—Vivaldi's music reflects the joys of *Spring*, highly changeable, with gentle breezes punctuated by brief thundering interludes. *Summer* is depicted as hot, humid, and somnolent; the music, slow and leisurely, is interspersed with the sounds of thunderstorms more violent and longer lasting than those heard in the spring. The music of *Autumn* is lively and happy, signifying pleasant weather and the joyful activities of harvesting and wine tasting. Vivaldi tells about the bitter cold of *Winter* through music portraying shivering bodies and chattering teeth. When reflecting the comfort of relaxation in front of a warm fire, the music becomes slower and takes on a mellow quality.

Other musicians who have written "climatic music" are Gregor Werner, whose *Curious Musical Instrumental Calendar* depicts month-to-month changes of weather, and Franz Joseph Haydn, who composed the oratorio *The Seasons*. Guiseppe Verdi created a ballet sequence with the same name for his opera *Sicilian Vespers*. Alexander Glazunov also composed a ballet called *The Seasons*, which starts with winter and progresses around the calendar. The music and dancers begin slowly during the cold, dreary Russian winter and build to a rousing, happy finale during the autumn.

Seasonal weather is reflected in such well-known music as Igor Stravinsky's *Rite of Spring*, Edward Grieg's soprano solo "Autumn Song," and Peter Ilyich Tchaikovsky's First Symphony, subtitled "Winter Dreams."

Many musical creations have been inspired by weather events ranging from the calmness of a gentle rain to the excitement of a violent thunderstorm. As might be expected, the sudden brilliance of lightning and the crashes of thunder have been portrayed by many composers. In his Sixth Symphony (*Pastoral*), Ludwig van Beethoven accurately conveys the atmosphere of a spring day and the gradual development of a thunderstorm. The music builds furiously, with faster notes representing heavy rain; strong winds punish the trees and the sound of thunder explodes. The music ends with the dissipating storm moving away toward the east and a beautiful rainbow appearing in the sky.

Many other composers have included the sounds and emotions of thunderstorms in their music. In his *Grand Canyon Suite*, Ferde Grofé features a storm of grand ferocity. Hector Berlioz, in the third movement of his *Fantastic Symphony*, uses four kettledrums (timpani) tuned to different pitches to create realistically the rumble of thunder (Figure 13-1).

A hailstorm is included in Handel's oratorio *Israel in Egypt*. Frédéric Chopin wrote the "Raindrop" prelude (Prelude no. 15), Hugo Alfvén composed "Summer Rain," while Camille Saint-Saëns's little-known oratorio, *The Flood*, glorifies the inundation that made Noah famous.

190

Figure 13-1 Rumbles of thunder occur three times in measures 175 to 191 of the third movement of the *Fantastic Symphony*, by Hector Berlioz. (From *The Symphony*, Paul Henry Lang, ed. Reprinted with permission of W. W. Norton and Co., Inc.)

The winds were given special attention by Claude Debussy in his preludes "The Wind in the Plain" and "What the West Wind Saw." Modest Mussorgsky composed a baritone solo called "The Winds are Howling."

POPULAR MUSIC

The composers of popular music also have found inspiration in the sky. McHugh and Fields advised us to leave our troubles on the doorstep and get our feet "On the Sunny Side of the Street." But sometimes the sun does not shine, and, as Burt Bacharach and Hal David wrote, "Raindrops Keep Falling on My Head." Gene Kelly never let that bother him as he danced with joy while "Singing in the Rain." In Hollywood, the occasions for such activity are not too frequent: According to Albert Hammond, "It Never Rains in Southern California." This is mostly true for the summer, but during some winters it really pours.

Most of us have fond memories of Judy Garland's rendition of "Over the Rainbow," Lena Horne's "Stormy Weather," and Bing Crosby's, "White Christmas." The list of melodies connected with the weather is seemingly endless.

PAINTERS VIEW THE SKIES

People and the substantial forms surrounding them are the central features of the paintings sometimes called "classical landscapes," which date back to very early artists. In such landscapes, the sights, lights, and motions of the atmosphere were generally not treated as essential, integral parts of the total scene (although clouds were often part of the pictorial structure). Sometimes—and in most landscapes since the seventeenth century—the atmosphere has been used to create a mood.

Naturalistic landscape painting as we know it today had its beginnings in sixteenth-century Germany and extended through the following century, particularly in Holland. But it was not until about 1800 that naturalistic landscape painting gained a secure place in the museums and salons of the art world. John Constable (1770–1837) is often cited as the person most responsible for this new perception. His work gained the admiration and attention of connoisseurs in his homeland and continental Europe (Figure 13-2).

Figure 13-2 *Vale of Dedham,* by John Constable.
(Courtesy of the National Gallery of Scotland, Edinburgh.)

Figure 13-3 *Hunters in the Snow,* by Pieter Brueghel the Elder. (Courtesy of Kunsthistorisches Museum, Vienna.)

Of course, there were many earlier artists who had incorporated the realities of nature in their paintings and who inspired Constable. In the development of his distinctive style, Constable profited from studies of the works of Titian, Claude Lorraine, and others. He surely was familiar with the Flemish painters and may have been influenced by such early landscapes as *Hunters in the Snow,* one of a set of six "seasonal paintings" done in the sixteenth century by Pieter Brueghel the Elder (Figure 13-3). J. M. W. Turner, Constable's contemporary in England, was widely regarded as another giant of natural landscaping. His dramatic scenes of tempestuous sea and sky are justifiably famous (Figure 13-4).

A modern painter following the traditions of Turner, Constable, and their predecessors sees much more in a landscape than the rocks and trees, rivers and streams, mountains and valleys, and living creatures that inhabit the land: The artist also sees the sky as part of the whole—not a blank space, but an integral feature of the total landscape that contributes to the mood, the emotion, and the central theme of the painting.

A landscape painter must see and "feel" the atmosphere—the quality of the light; the character of the wind; the types and movements of clouds; rain and snow; and optical phenomena such as rainbows and halos. The location and the quality of brightness and shadows are of vital importance.

Constable was particularly interested—almost obsessed—with what he called the chiaroscuro—that is, the light and dark—of nature. He was a master at highlighting the brilliant sparkle of sunlight reflecting from dew drops, fresh flowers, or the surfaces of wet leaves. Constable realized these touches of "chiaro" through the use of pure white applied with a palette knife.

The most common rendering of the concept of chiaroscuro is found in the use of light and dark to give paintings a greater sense of form and space and an enhanced sense of drama. A large thundercloud brilliantly illuminated on one side and with deep shadows on the other is given life through the meaningful use of lights and darks, which also give the picture a greater sense of depth.

Constable was interested in the physical origins of clouds, dew, rainbows, and other meteorological phenomena. He was aware of the still-used cloud-classification system developed in England by Luke Howard in 1803. It is no wonder that Constable, who combined his enormous artistic talent and expertise in atmospheric phenomena and processes, is known as the foremost of meteorological artists.

The German Romantic painter of the nineteenth century Casper David Friedrich did many "weather pictures." Most of them show a keen sense of observation and are very realistic but are intended as religious allegories.

Figure 13-4 *The Storm*, by J. M. W. Turner. (Courtesy of the British Museum, London.)

Over the years, many painters in many countries, including the United States, have carried forward and extended the concepts emphasized by Constable. The Hudson River School included many outstanding landscape painters.

A number of American artists have been perceptive observers of the weather and its effects. One of them, Charles M. Russell, was a cowboy employed by a large cattle company. During the winter of 1886, Montana experienced the most severe snowstorm in its history, which took a heavy toll of cattle under Russell's care. When his employers sought an explanation, Russell's response was the watercolor *Waiting for a Chinook*, a painting that was to make him famous (Figure 13-5). Not only did it show the tragic condition of the range and the steers, but the title indicated that Russell knew the solution was the arrival of the warm chinook winds that would increase temperatures and melt the snow.

Eric Sloane, a present-day American artist, deserves particular mention because of his dedication to the art of the atmosphere and his effectiveness in teaching others about the weather. Following in the footsteps of Constable, he decided that before he could properly paint clouds, he first had

Figure 13-5 *Waiting for a Chinook,* by Charles M. Russell. (Courtesy of Buffalo Bill Historical Center, Cody, Wyoming.)

Figure 13-6 *Sun Shafts,* by Eric Sloane. (From *For Spacious Skies,* Thomas Y. Crowell, 1978; with permission of Eric Sloane.)

to know about their "anatomy." In 1930, he enrolled in a short course in meteorology at the Massachusetts Institute of Technology. It was the beginning of an experience of learning and teaching that spanned more than five decades and produced a long series of highly illustrated books as well as many magnificent paintings (Figure 13-6). Sloane's landscapes are rich in meteorological detail and reflect the talent and knowledge of the artist. They satisfy the eye and are lessons in nature.

A CARICATURIST AND THE WEATHER

Almost all of the approximately 1000 plates etched by English caricaturist James Gillray (1756–1815) were angry political notices or satirical commentaries on contemporary society. But among the etchings he left behind

Figure 13-7 *Very Slippy-Weather* by James Gillray. (Courtesy of American Meteorological Society, Boston.)

were nine well-known works in which the weather is the principal theme: *Delicious Weather, Dreadful Hot Weather, Sad Sloppy Weather, Raw Weather, Fire Bracing Weather, Windy Weather, A Squall, A Clam,* and *Very Slippy-Weather* (Figure 13-7).

Gillray's impressions humorously depict the effects of daily weather on the lives of Londoners. Unlike the paintings of Constable, who lived at

Figure 13-8   "Frost fair" on the frozen Thames River in London during the winter of 1683–1684. (Courtesy of BBC Hulton Picture Library, London, England.)

the same time, Gillray's drawings do not have the beauty and attention to meteorological detail displayed in Constable's paintings, but they inspire a chuckle or two and remind us of the joys and pains of the weather. Copies of these etchings can be seen at the American Meteorological Society, 45 Beacon Street, Boston.

ART RECORDS THE CLIMATE

Climatologists have found that paintings and etchings, some rendered in the distant past, are fruitful sources of climatic information. In *Climate: Present, Past and Future*, English climatologist H. H. Lamb shows a cave painting dating back to 3500 BC at Aounet, in the Sahara Desert. The painting depicts a hunter in a canoe in search of a hippopotamus and strongly suggests that it was much wetter in the area now occupied by the Sahara.

Lamb also uses Brueghel's *Hunters in the Snow*, painted in February 1565, as an illustration of a particularly severe winter in Flanders that occurred early in a centuries-long period of very cold weather throughout Europe. The extremity of the cold during the winter of 1683–1684 is demonstrated by a picture of a fair on the frozen Thames River in London (Figure 13-8). According to Lamb, there are many pictures of the icebound Thames during the eighteenth century.

These observations verify the existence of the Little Ice Age that extended from about 1500 to 1900. Additional evidence of this cold period is found in pictures of Alpine scenes depicting the extent of glaciers. During cold, snowy winters, a glacier, behaving like a massive river of ice, advances downhill slowly. During warm intervals, the glacier retreats as the forward extensions of the ice melt and evaporate.

In *Times of Fear, Times of Feast*, published in 1971, Le Roy Ladurie presents a series of engravings and drawings showing the extent of the Grindelwald glacier in Switzerland. In 1640 it was "swollen bristling with séracs, stretched far beyond its present positions." Artists' renderings in 1686, 1720, 1748, and about 1778 continued to show the glacier in a very advanced position, almost reaching the main Grindelwald Valley and threatening a village at the mouth of the gorge that contained the glacier. A photograph taken in 1966 at the village shows that the glacier has retreated to higher elevations and no longer fills the Grindelwald gorge as it did in the seventeenth, eighteenth, and nineteenth centuries.

According to engravings in the Bibliotèque Nationale, a massive glacier occupied the Rhône Valley in Switzerland during the eighteenth century. By 1966 it had retreated into the high country, leaving the lower valley ice-free with the Muttbach River carrying water down to the Rhône. Similar sequences of events can be shown to have occurred in other Alpine valleys, providing evidence that the cold period of several centuries' duration ended early in the twentieth century and was followed by a prolonged warm period still existing today.

The pictorial evidence supports and supplements the instrumental evidence, illustrating a point not generally recognized: In addition to serving many masters, art also records the natural history of the earth.

Postscript

In enumerating how the atmosphere influences what we do and how we do it, the list of subjects could go on and on. For example, there could have been chapters on sports, business, animal health and behavior, and game and commercial fishing. These subjects will have to be dealt with at a later date.

As noted at the outset, this volume was not intended to be a comprehensive treatment on how the weather and the climate affect human affairs. Instead, the intent has been to introduce you to the subject. Interested readers who want to know more can consult the bibliography in Appendix III.

A closing thought to remember: There is no way to guarantee health, happiness, and personal fulfillment, but a wise person seeks to maximize the chances of their occurrence. Since the atmosphere is one of the important terms in the human equation, it should be factored into decisions that govern your life.

Climatic Data—United States and Canada

CLIMATIC DATA—UNITED STATES AND CANADA*

T—normal daily average temperature (°F)
P—normal monthly precipitation (inches)
N—number of days with 0.01 or more inches of precipitation
S—snowfall (including ice pellets)(inches), t means *trace*

		J	F	M	A	M	J	J	A	S	O	N	D	Annual
Montgomery, Alabama	T	47	50	57	65	72	79	82	81	77	65	55	49	65
	P	4.2	4.5	5.9	4.4	4.0	3.5	4.8	3.2	4.7	2.3	3.0	4.8	49.2
	N	11	9	11	8	9	9	12	9	8	5	8	10	109
	S	0.3	0.1	t	0	0	0	0	0	0	0	t	t	0.4
Fairbanks, Alaska	T	−13	−4	8	30	48	59	62	57	45	25	4	−10	26
	P	0.5	0.4	0.4	0.3	0.6	1.3	1.8	1.9	1.1	0.7	0.7	0.7	10.4
	N	7	6	7	5	6	10	12	12	9	10	9	8	101
	S	10.1	9.0	7.2	3.5	0.6	t	0	t	1.1	10.2	12.5	12.4	66.6
Phoenix, Arizona	T	52	56	61	68	77	86	92	90	85	73	61	53	71
	P	0.7	0.6	0.8	0.3	0.1	0.2	0.7	1.0	0.6	0.6	0.5	0.8	7.1
	N	4	4	3	2	1	1	4	5	3	3	2	4	36
	S	t	t	t	t	0	0	0	0	0	0	0	t	t
Little Rock, Arkansas	T	40	44	52	62	70	78	82	81	74	63	51	43	62
	P	3.9	3.8	4.7	5.4	5.3	3.7	3.6	3.1	4.3	2.8	4.4	4.2	49.2
	N	10	9	11	10	10	8	9	7	7	6	8	9	104
	S	2.3	1.5	0.5	t	0	0	0	0	0	0	0.3	0.9	5.5

*Arranged alphabetically by state or province.

		J	F	M	A	M	J	J	A	S	O	N	D	Annual
Los Angeles, California	T	57	59	60	62	65	69	74	75	73	69	63	58	65
	P	3.7	3.0	2.4	1.2	0.2	0.03	0.0	0.1	0.3	0.2	1.8	2.0	14.8
	N	6	5	6	4	1	1	0	1	1	2	3	5	35
	S	t	t	0	0	0	0	0	0	0	0	0	t	t
San Francisco, California	T	48	52	53	55	58	61	62	63	64	61	54	49	57
	P	4.6	3.2	2.6	1.5	0.3	0.1	0.03	0.05	0.2	1.1	2.4	3.6	19.7
	N	11	10	10	6	3	1	1	1	1	4	8	10	66
	S	t	t	t	0	0	0	0	0	0	0	0	t	t
Denver, Colorado	T	30	34	38	47	57	67	73	71	63	52	39	33	50
	P	0.5	0.7	1.2	1.8	2.5	1.6	1.9	1.5	1.2	1.0	0.8	0.6	15.3
	N	6	6	9	9	10	9	9	9	6	5	5	5	88
	S	8.1	7.7	12.7	9.4	1.9	t	0	0	1.6	3.7	8.0	6.5	59.6
Hartford, Connecticut	T	25	28	37	49	59	69	73	71	63	52	42	29	50
	P	3.5	3.2	4.2	4.0	3.4	3.4	3.1	4.0	3.9	3.5	4.0	4.2	44.4
	N	11	10	12	11	11	11	10	10	10	8	11	12	127
	S	12.2	12.6	11.5	1.5	0.1	0	0	0	0	0.1	2.0	11.9	51.9
Wilmington, Delaware	T	31	33	42	52	62	71	76	75	68	56	46	36	54
	P	3.1	3.0	3.9	3.4	3.2	3.5	3.9	4.0	3.6	2.9	3.3	3.5	41.4
	N	11	9	11	11	12	10	9	9	8	8	10	10	118
	S	6.2	6.4	3.8	0.1	t	0	0	0	0	0.1	1.1	3.6	21.3
Washington, D.C.	T	35	37	46	56	65	73	78	77	70	58	48	38	57
	P	3.2	2.8	3.8	3.4	3.9	4.0	4.2	5.1	3.6	3.2	3.1	3.4	43.5
	N	11	9	11	10	11	9	10	9	8	7	8	9	112
	S	4.9	5.5	2.5	t	t	0	0	0	0	t	0.7	3.4	17.0

		J	F	M	A	M	J	J	A	S	O	N	D	Annual
Miami, Florida	T	67	68	72	75	78	81	82	83	82	78	73	68	76
	P	2.1	2.0	1.9	3.1	6.5	9.2	6.0	7.0	8.1	7.1	2.7	1.9	57.6
	N	7	6	5	6	11	15	16	17	17	15	8	7	130
	S	0	0	0	0	0	0	0	0	0	0	0	0	0
Atlanta, Georgia	T	42	45	52	62	69	76	79	78	73	62	52	44	61
	P	4.9	4.4	5.9	4.4	4.0	3.4	4.7	3.4	3.2	2.5	3.4	4.2	48.6
	N	12	10	12	9	9	10	12	9	8	6	8	10	115
	S	0.7	0.5	0.3	t	0	0	0	0	0	0	t	0.2	1.7
Honolulu, Hawaii	T	73	73	74	76	78	79	80	81	80	80	77	74	77
	P	3.8	2.7	3.5	1.5	1.2	0.5	0.5	0.6	0.6	1.9	3.2	3.4	23.5
	N	10	10	9	9	7	6	8	7	7	9	9	10	101
	S	0	0	0	0	0	0	0	0	0	0	0	0	0
Boise, Idaho	T	30	36	41	49	57	66	75	72	63	52	40	32	51
	P	1.6	1.1	1.0	1.2	1.2	1.0	0.3	0.4	0.6	0.8	1.3	1.3	11.7
	N	13	11	9	8	8	6	2	3	4	6	10	11	91
	S	7.4	3.9	2.0	0.7	0.1	t	0	0	0	0.1	1.9	5.1	21.2
Chicago, Illinois	T	21	26	36	49	59	69	73	72	65	54	40	28	49
	P	1.6	1.3	2.6	3.7	3.2	4.1	3.6	3.5	3.4	2.3	2.1	2.1	33.4
	N	11	10	13	13	11	10	10	9	10	9	10	11	127
	S	11.1	7.8	7.4	1.8	0.1	0	0	0	t	0.4	2.2	9.4	40.2
Indianapolis, Indiana	T	26	30	40	52	62	72	75	73	67	55	42	32	52
	P	2.6	2.5	3.6	3.7	3.7	4.0	4.3	3.5	2.7	2.5	3.0	3.0	39.1

		J	F	M	A	M	J	J	A	S	O	N	D	Annual
Indianapolis (cont.)	N	12	10	13	12	12	10	9	9	8	8	10	11	124
	S	6.0	5.4	3.7	0.5	t	0	0	0	0	t	2.1	4.7	22.4
Des Moines, Iowa	T	19	24	35	50	62	72	76	74	65	54	39	26	50
	P	1.0	1.1	2.2	3.2	4.0	4.2	3.2	4.1	3.1	2.2	1.5	1.0	30.8
	N	8	7	10	10	11	11	9	9	9	7	6	7	104
	S	8.5	7.2	6.8	1.7	t	0	0	0	t	0.3	2.6	6.3	33.4
Topeka, Kansas	T	26	32	42	55	65	74	79	77	68	57	43	32	54
	P	0.9	1.0	2.2	3.1	4.0	5.1	4.0	3.7	3.4	2.8	1.8	1.3	33.4
	N	6	6	8	10	11	10	9	8	7	6	6	6	93
	S	6.0	4.6	4.5	0.6	0	0	0	0	0	t	1.2	4.7	21.6
Louisville, Kentucky	T	32	36	45	57	65	74	78	76	70	58	46	37	56
	P	3.4	3.2	4.7	4.1	4.2	3.6	4.1	3.3	3.4	2.6	3.5	3.5	43.6
	N	12	11	13	12	11	10	11	8	8	7	10	11	124
	S	6.3	4.4	3.9	0.1	0	0	0	0	0	t	1.4	2.2	18.3
Baton Rouge, Louisiana	T	52	54	60	68	75	80	82	81	78	68	59	53	68
	P	4.6	5.0	4.6	5.6	4.8	3.1	7.1	5.0	4.4	2.6	4.0	5.0	55.8
	N	10	9	9	7	8	9	14	12	9	5	7	10	109
	S	t	0.2	t	0	0	0	0	0	0	0	t	t	0.2
Portland, Maine	T	22	23	32	43	53	62	68	67	59	48	38	26	45
	P	3.8	3.6	4.0	3.9	3.3	3.1	2.8	2.8	3.3	3.8	4.7	4.5	43.5
	N	11	10	11	12	12	11	9	9	8	9	12	11	125
	S	19.3	18.7	13.3	2.9	0.2	0	0	0	t	0.3	3.4	15.7	73.8

		J	F	M	A	M	J	J	A	S	O	N	D	Annual
Baltimore, Maryland	T	33	35	43	54	63	72	77	76	69	57	46	36	55
	P	2.9	2.9	3.7	3.4	3.4	3.9	3.9	4.6	3.5	3.1	3.1	3.4	41.8
	N	10	9	11	11	11	9	9	10	7	7	9	9	112
	S	5.3	6.9	4.6	0.1	t	0	0	0	0	t	1.1	3.9	21.9
Boston, Massachusetts	T	30	31	38	49	59	68	74	72	65	55	45	34	52
	P	3.9	3.7	4.1	3.7	3.5	2.9	2.7	3.7	3.4	3.4	4.2	4.5	43.8
	N	12	11	12	11	11	10	9	10	9	9	11	11	126
	S	12.4	11.9	8.0	0.7	t	0	0	0	0	t	1.2	7.8	42.0
Detroit, Michigan	T	23	26	35	48	58	68	72	70	63	52	40	28	49
	P	1.9	1.7	2.5	3.2	2.8	3.4	3.1	3.2	2.2	2.1	2.3	2.5	40.0
	N	13	12	13	12	12	11	9	9	9	9	11	13	133
	S	7.9	7.7	5.4	1.1	t	0	0	0	0	t	2.5	7.1	31.7
Minneapolis, Minnesota	T	11	18	29	46	58	68	73	71	61	50	33	19	45
	P	0.8	0.8	1.7	2.0	3.2	4.1	3.5	3.6	2.5	1.8	1.3	0.9	26.4
	N	9	7	10	10	11	12	10	10	9	8	8	9	113
	S	9.4	8.3	10.6	2.6	0.2	0	0	0	t	0.4	6.0	8.9	46.4
Jackson, Mississippi	T	46	49	56	65	73	79	82	81	76	65	55	49	65
	P	5.0	4.5	5.9	5.8	4.8	2.9	4.4	3.7	3.6	2.6	4.2	5.4	52.8
	N	12	8	11	9	9	7	11	10	9	5	8	10	109
	S	0.5	0.2	0.3	t	0	0	0	0	0	0	t	t	1.0
Springfield, Missouri	T	32	36	45	56	65	73	78	77	70	58	45	36	56
	P	1.6	2.1	3.4	4.0	4.3	4.7	3.6	2.8	4.2	3.2	2.9	2.6	39.5

		J	F	M	A	M	J	J	A	S	O	N	D	Annual
Springfield (cont.)	N	9	8	10	11	11	10	8	8	8	7	8	9	107
	S	3.9	4.1	3.7	0.5	0	0	0	0	0	t	2.1	2.3	16.6
Helena, Montana	T	18	26	32	42	52	60	68	66	56	45	31	24	43
	P	0.6	0.4	0.7	1.1	1.7	2.0	1.0	1.2	1.8	0.6	0.5	0.6	11.4
	N	9	7	8	8	11	12	7	8	7	6	7	8	98
	S	9.4	6.3	7.5	5.2	1.4	0.1	t	0	1.3	1.9	6.8	8.6	48.5
Omaha, Nebraska	T	21	27	37	52	63	73	78	75	66	56	40	27	51
	P	0.8	1.9	1.9	2.9	4.3	4.0	3.6	4.1	3.5	2.1	1.3	0.8	30.3
	N	7	7	9	10	12	10	9	9	8	6	5	6	98
	S	8.3	7.2	6.7	0.9	0.1	0	0	0	t	0.4	2.4	5.6	31.6
Las Vegas, Nevada	T	45	50	55	64	73	84	90	88	80	68	54	45	66
	P	0.5	0.5	0.4	0.2	0.2	0.1	0.4	0.5	0.3	0.2	0.4	0.3	4.2
	N	3	3	3	2	1	1	3	3	2	2	2	2	27
	S	1.4	t	t	t	0	0	0	0	0	t	0.2	0.1	1.7
Concord, New Hampshire	T	20	22	32	44	55	65	70	67	59	48	37	24	45
	P	2.8	2.5	2.9	3.0	2.9	2.9	2.9	3.3	3.1	3.1	3.7	3.4	36.5
	N	11	9	11	11	12	11	10	10	9	8	11	11	124
	S	18.0	14.9	11.2	2.2	0.2	0	0	0	0	0.1	4.1	13.9	64.6
Newark, New Jersey	T	31	33	41	52	62	72	77	76	68	57	46	36	54
	P	3.1	3.0	4.2	3.6	3.6	2.9	3.8	4.3	3.7	3.1	3.6	3.4	42.3
	N	11	10	11	11	12	10	10	9	8	8	10	11	120
	S	7.4	8.6	5.0	0.5	t	0	0	0	0	t	0.5	6.4	28.4

		J	F	M	A	M	J	J	A	S	O	N	D	Annual
Albuquerque, New Mexico	T	35	39	45	55	64	73	77	75	68	58	44	38	56
	P	0.4	0.4	0.5	0.4	0.5	0.5	1.3	1.5	0.8	0.9	0.4	0.5	8.1
	N	4	4	4	3	4	4	9	9	6	5	3	4	59
	S	2.4	2.0	2.0	0.5	t	0	0	0	t	t	1.2	2.7	10.8
New York, New York	T	32	33	41	52	62	71	77	75	68	58	47	36	54
	P	3.2	3.1	4.2	3.8	3.8	3.2	3.8	4.0	3.7	3.4	4.1	3.8	44.1
	N	11	10	12	11	11	10	10	10	8	8	9	10	120
	S	7.6	8.8	5.1	0.9	t	0	0	0	0	t	0.9	5.7	29.0
Raleigh, North Carolina	T	40	42	49	60	67	74	78	77	71	60	50	42	59
	P	3.6	3.4	3.7	2.9	3.7	3.7	4.4	4.4	3.3	2.7	2.9	3.1	41.8
	N	10	10	11	9	10	9	11	10	8	7	8	9	112
	S	2.5	2.6	1.6	t	0	0	0	0	0	0	0.2	0.9	7.8
Bismarck, North Dakota	T	7	14	26	42	55	64	70	69	57	46	29	15	41
	P	0.5	0.4	0.7	1.5	2.2	3.0	2.0	2.0	1.7	0.8	0.5	0.5	15.4
	N	8	7	8	8	10	12	9	8	7	5	6	8	96
	S	7.1	6.5	8.0	3.7	1.0	t	0	0	0.2	1.2	5.1	6.6	39.4
Cleveland, Ohio	T	26	27	37	48	58	68	72	70	64	53	42	31	50
	P	2.5	2.2	3.0	3.3	3.3	3.5	3.4	3.4	2.9	2.4	2.8	2.8	35.4
	N	16	14	16	14	13	11	10	10	10	11	14	16	155
	S	11.7	11.3	9.5	2.0	0.1	0	0	0	t	0.7	5.5	11.2	52.0
Oklahoma City, Oklahoma	T	36	41	49	60	68	77	82	81	73	62	49	40	60
	P	1.0	1.3	2.1	2.9	5.5	3.9	3.0	2.4	3.4	2.7	1.5	1.2	30.9

		J	F	M	A	M	J	J	A	S	O	N	D	Annual
Oklahoma City (cont.)	N	5	6	7	8	10	9	7	6	7	6	5	5	81
	S	2.9	2.5	1.6	t	0	0	0	0	0	t	0.5	1.5	9.0
Portland, Oregon	T	39	43	46	50	57	62	68	67	63	54	46	41	53
	P	6.2	3.9	3.6	2.3	2.1	1.5	0.5	1.3	1.6	3.0	5.2	6.4	37.4
	N	19	16	17	14	12	9	4	5	8	13	18	19	154
	S	4.2	0.7	0.5	t	t	0	0	0	t	t	0.5	1.4	7.3
Pittsburgh, Pennsylvania	T	27	29	38	50	60	68	72	71	64	52	42	31	50
	P	2.9	2.4	3.6	3.3	3.5	3.3	3.8	3.3	2.8	2.5	2.3	2.6	36.3
	N	17	14	16	13	12	11	11	10	9	10	13	16	152
	S	12.4	10.1	8.7	1.4	0.2	0	0	0	0	0.2	4.1	8.2	45.3
Providence, Rhode Island	T	28	29	37	48	58	67	72	71	64	53	43	32	50
	P	4.1	3.7	4.3	4.0	3.5	2.8	3.0	4.0	3.5	3.8	4.2	4.5	45.3
	M	11	10	12	11	11	11	9	10	8	8	11	12	124
	S	9.6	10.5	8.8	0.6	0.3	0	0	0	0	0.2	0.7	7.0	37.7
Columbia, South Carolina	T	45	47	54	64	72	78	81	80	75	63	54	47	63
	P	4.3	4.0	5.2	3.6	3.8	4.4	5.4	5.6	4.2	2.6	2.5	3.5	49.1
	N	10	10	11	8	9	10	12	11	8	6	7	9	111
	S	0.3	1.0	0.3	0	0	0	0	0	0	0	t	0.3	1.9
Rapid City, South Dakota	T	21	26	33	45	56	65	73	71	61	50	35	26	47
	P	0.4	0.6	1.0	2.0	2.6	3.3	2.1	1.4	1.0	0.8	0.5	0.4	16.3
	N	7	8	9	10	12	12	9	8	6	5	5	6	98
	S	5.3	6.6	9.2	5.9	0.8	0.1	0	0	0.1	1.6	4.5	4.7	38.8

		J	F	M	A	M	J	J	A	S	O	N	D	Annual
Nashville, Tennessee	T	37	40	49	60	68	76	79	78	72	60	49	41	59
	P	4.5	4.0	5.6	4.5	4.6	3.7	3.8	3.4	3.7	2.6	3.5	4.6	48.5
	N	12	11	12	11	11	9	10	9	8	7	9	11	120
	S	4.2	3.2	1.7	0.1	0	0	0	0	0	0	0.6	1.8	11.6
Dallas–Fort Worth, Texas	T	44	48	56	66	74	82	86	86	79	68	56	48	66
	P	1.6	1.9	2.4	3.6	4.3	2.6	2.0	1.8	3.3	2.5	1.8	1.7	29.4
	N	7	7	7	8	8	6	5	5	7	5	6	6	77
	S	1.6	1.2	0.3	0	0	0	0	0	0	0	0.2	0.2	3.5
Houston, Texas	T	52	55	61	69	75	81	83	83	78	70	60	54	68
	P	3.2	3.2	2.7	4.2	4.7	4.0	3.3	3.7	4.9	3.7	3.4	3.7	44.8
	N	11	7	10	7	8	7	10	11	10	7	8	8	104
	S	0.2	0.2	t	0	0	0	0	0	0	0	t	t	0.4
Salt Lake City, Utah	T	29	34	41	49	59	68	77	75	65	53	40	30	52
	P	1.4	1.3	1.7	2.2	1.5	1.0	0.7	0.9	0.9	1.1	1.2	1.4	15.3
	N	10	9	10	10	8	5	4	6	5	6	7	9	89
	S	13.5	9.7	10.4	4.9	0.6	t	0	0	0.1	1.0	6.4	11.7	58.3
Burlington, Vermont	T	17	18	29	43	55	65	70	67	59	48	37	23	44
	P	1.8	1.7	2.2	2.7	3.0	3.6	3.4	3.9	3.2	2.8	2.8	2.4	33.7
	N	14	12	13	12	13	12	12	12	12	11	14	15	152
	S	18.7	17.1	12.2	3.6	0.2	0	0	0	t	0.2	7.3	19.3	78.6
Richmond, Virginia	T	37	39	47	58	66	74	78	77	70	59	49	40	58
	P	3.2	3.1	3.6	2.9	3.6	3.6	5.1	5.0	3.5	3.7	3.3	3.4	44.1

		J	F	M	A	M	J	J	A	S	O	N	D	Annual
Richmond (cont.)	N	11	9	11	9	11	9	11	10	8	7	8	9	113
	S	5.2	3.8	3.1	0.1	0	0	0	0	0	t	0.4	2.0	14.6
Seattle, Washington	T	41	44	46	50	56	61	65	65	61	54	46	43	53
	P	5.9	4.2	3.7	2.5	1.7	1.5	0.9	1.4	2.0	3.4	5.4	6.3	39.9
	N	19	16	17	14	10	9	5	6	9	10	18	20	153
	S	3.9	0.8	0.7	t	t	0	0	0	0	t	0.6	2.1	8.1
Charleston, West Virginia	T	33	36	45	55	64	71	75	74	68	56	45	37	55
	P	3.5	3.1	4.0	3.5	3.7	3.3	5.4	4.2	3.0	2.6	2.9	3.3	42.4
	N	16	14	15	14	13	11	13	11	9	10	12	14	152
	S	10.5	8.4	4.8	0.4	t	0	0	0	0	0.2	2.7	4.9	31.9
Madison, Wisconsin	T	16	20	31	46	57	66	70	68	60	50	35	22	45
	P	1.1	1.0	2.2	3.1	3.3	4.3	3.9	3.8	3.1	2.2	1.8	1.5	30.8
	N	10	8	11	11	11	11	9	10	9	8	9	10	117
	S	9.4	7.0	8.9	2.1	t	0	0	0	t	0.1	3.2	10.1	40.8
Cheyenne, Wyoming	T	26	29	32	42	52	62	69	67	58	48	35	29	46
	P	0.4	0.4	1.0	1.2	2.4	2.0	1.9	1.4	1.0	0.7	0.5	0.4	13.3
	N	6	6	9	10	12	11	11	9	7	5	6	5	97
	S	6.5	5.7	12.0	8.9	3.7	0.3	0	0	0.7	3.3	6.6	5.6	53.3
Edmonton, Alberta	T	6	13	22	39	52	58	64	61	52	42	24	13	37
	P	1.0	0.8	0.7	0.9	1.5	2.9	3.3	2.8	1.4	0.7	0.7	0.8	17.6
	N	12	10	10	8	9	12	13	12	9	6	9	11	121
	S	10.5	8.6	6.7	5.6	1.1	t	0	0	0.7	3.2	6.6	9.0	52.0

		J	F	M	A	M	J	J	A	S	O	N	D	Annual
Prince George, British Columbia	T	11	21	28	39	49	55	59	57	50	40	27	18	37
	P	2.3	1.7	1.2	1.2	1.7	2.3	2.3	2.9	2.2	2.4	2.2	2.1	24.4
	N	17	13	12	10	11	13	13	13	12	15	16	17	162
	S	23.4	14.7	9.8	4.0	0.8	t	0	0	0.4	4.0	15.5	19.3	91.9
Churchill, Manitoba	T	-18	-16	-5	12	28	43	54	53	42	30	11	7	19
	P	0.6	0.5	0.7	1.0	1.1	1.6	1.9	2.3	2.0	1.6	1.6	0.8	15.6
	N	10	9	10	11	11	9	11	12	14	15	17	12	141
	S	6.0	5.4	7.1	9.3	7.1	1.1	t	0	1.7	10.3	16.4	8.2	72.6
Fredericton, New Brunswick	T	15	17	27	39	51	60	66	64	56	46	35	21	42
	P	3.6	3.4	2.9	3.2	3.4	3.4	3.6	3.4	3.4	3.6	4.7	4.2	42.7
	N	12	10	11	12	13	12	12	12	10	11	13	12	140
	S	21.9	23.2	14.9	6.3	0.4	0	0	0	0	1.0	7.4	20.8	95.9
Goose Bay, Newfoundland	T	3	6	17	29	41	52	60	58	50	38	26	10	32
	P	2.7	2.4	2.7	2.1	2.4	3.2	4.0	3.6	3.0	2.8	2.8	2.7	34.5
	N	16	13	15	13	13	15	16	16	14	14	15	16	176
	S	28.0	22.8	27.8	17.1	6.9	0.7	0	0	1.0	9.8	20.7	26.3	161.1
Frobisher Bay, Northwest Territories	T	-15	-13	-8	7	26	38	46	44	36	24	10	-5	16
	P	1.0	1.1	0.8	0.9	0.9	1.5	2.1	2.3	1.7	1.6	1.4	1.0	16.3
	N	10	11	9	9	10	10	11	11	13	14	12	12	132
	S	10.1	11.4	8.5	9.3	8.5	3.3	0.1	0.1	5.7	14.2	14.9	11.1	97.3
Resolute, Northwest Territories	T	-27	-28	-24	-10	13	31	40	37	23	6	-12	-20	2
	P	0.1	0.1	0.1	0.2	0.3	0.5	1.0	1.2	0.7	0.6	0.2	0.2	5.4

		J	F	M	A	M	J	J	A	S	O	N	D	Annual
Resolute (cont.)	N	5	5	5	6	9	7	9	10	11	14	7	6	94
	S	1.1	1.3	1.3	2.3	3.5	2.6	1.2	1.9	5.6	6.1	2.2	1.9	31.0
Yellowknife, Northwest Territories	T	−19	−14	−1	18	39	54	61	57	44	30	6	−11	22
	P	0.5	0.5	0.5	0.4	0.6	0.7	1.3	1.4	1.1	1.2	0.9	0.7	9.8
	N	10	10	9	6	5	6	9	10	10	11	14	14	114
	S	5.8	5.2	5.1	3.5	1.0	0.1	0	0	1.0	7.3	10.1	7.9	47.0
Halifax, Nova Scotia	T	25	24	31	39	48	57	64	64	59	50	41	30	44
	P	5.8	5.1	4.4	4.2	4.3	3.4	3.6	3.7	3.7	4.5	6.0	5.8	54.4
	N	15	12	12	12	13	10	10	10	9	10	14	15	142
	S	18.7	21.0	15.8	4.7	0.4	0	0	0	0	0.1	2.7	15.7	79.1
Toronto, Ontario	T	24	25	33	46	56	67	71	70	63	52	41	29	48
	P	2.5	2.2	2.6	2.6	2.9	2.5	3.2	2.6	2.4	2.4	2.6	2.5	31.1
	N	15	12	12	12	12	9	9	9	9	9	13	13	134
	S	14.6	13.1	9.3	2.9	0.1	0	0	0	0	0.2	4.0	11.3	55.6
Charlottetown, Prince Edward Island	T	20	19	26	36	47	57	65	64	57	47	38	26	42
	P	3.8	3.2	3.0	2.9	3.1	3.1	2.9	3.6	3.6	3.9	4.5	3.9	41.7
	N	18	15	15	13	13	12	11	12	12	13	17	18	169
	S	29.1	25.8	20.4	10.2	0.7	0	0	0	0	0.4	7.0	25.7	120.1
Montreal, Quebec	T	16	18	29	44	56	66	71	69	60	50	37	22	45
	P	3.1	2.8	3.0	3.0	2.9	3.4	3.7	3.6	3.4	3.1	3.6	3.6	39.3
	N	17	15	13	13	13	12	13	12	12	12	15	17	164
	S	21.2	21.9	15.0	4.3	0.6	0	0	0	t	0.6	9.3	22.8	95.7

Appendix I

		J	F	M	A	M	J	J	A	S	O	N	D	Annual
Saskatoon, Saskatchewan	T	−2	5	16	37	51	60	66	63	52	41	22	7	35
	P	0.7	0.7	0.7	0.8	1.3	2.3	2.1	1.8	1.3	0.8	0.7	0.7	13.9
	N	11	9	9	7	7	10	10	9	8	6	8	9	103
	S	7.7	7.4	6.6	3.8	0.8	0	0	0	0.5	3.4	6.6	7.5	44.3
Whitehorse, Yukon Territory	T	−2	8	18	32	45	54	57	54	46	33	16	4	31
	P	0.7	0.6	0.6	0.4	0.5	1.1	1.3	1.4	1.1	0.8	0.9	0.8	10.2
	N	13	10	8	6	6	9	11	10	10	9	13	13	118
	S	8.1	5.9	6.5	4.2	1.1	0.2	0	0.1	1.5	5.4	9.1	8.2	50.3

Sources: Climatography of the United States, No. 81 (by State), National Climatic Center, Asheville, N.C., September 1982; and F. K. Hare and M. K. Thomas, Climate Canada, New York: Wiley, 1974.

Climatic Data—World

CLIMATIC DATA—WORLD

T—average temperature (°F)
P—average precipitation (inches; *t* means *trace*)

		J	F	M	A	M	J	J	A	S	O	N	D	Annual
Athens, Greece	T	47	48	53	59	67	75	80	80	74	66	57	51	63
	P	2.2	1.6	1.4	0.8	0.8	0.6	0.2	0.4	0.6	1.7	2.8	2.8	15.9
Beijing, P.R.C.	T	25	29	42	56	69	75	80	77	70	56	39	29	54
	P	0.1	0.2	0.2	0.6	1.5	3.4	8.3	6.1	2.5	0.7	0.3	0.1	24.1
Berlin, Germany	T	31	32	38	46	56	61	64	62	56	47	38	33	47
	P	1.9	1.3	1.5	1.7	1.9	2.3	3.1	2.2	1.9	1.7	1.7	1.9	23.1
Buenos Aires, Argentina	T	74	73	69	62	55	50	49	51	55	60	66	71	61
	P	3.1	2.8	4.3	3.5	3.0	2.4	2.2	2.4	3.1	3.4	3.3	3.9	37.4
Cairo, U.A.R.	T	54	56	61	68	75	80	81	81	77	72	65	57	69
	P	0.2	0.2	0.2	0.1	0.1	t	0.0	0.0	t	t	0.1	0.2	1.1
Delhi, India	T	58	62	74	86	92	92	86	85	84	79	68	60	77
	P	0.9	0.7	0.5	0.3	0.5	2.9	7.1	6.8	4.6	0.4	0.1	0.4	25.2
Jerusalem, Israel	T	47	48	55	61	69	73	75	75	73	69	62	52	63
	P	5.1	4.7	2.9	0.9	0.1	t	0.0	0.0	t	0.3	2.2	3.5	19.7
Lagos, Nigeria	T	81	83	83	83	82	79	78	78	79	80	82	82	81
	P	1.1	1.8	4.0	5.9	10.6	18.1	11.0	2.5	5.5	8.1	2.7	1.0	72.3

		J	F	M	A	M	J	J	A	S	O	N	D	Annual
London, U.K.	T	41	41	43	47	55	59	63	62	57	51	44	41	50
	P	2.0	1.5	1.4	1.8	1.8	1.6	2.0	2.2	1.8	2.3	2.5	2.0	22.9
Melbourne, Australia	T	67	68	65	59	54	50	49	51	54	58	61	65	59
	P	1.9	1.8	2.2	2.3	2.1	2.1	1.9	1.9	2.3	2.6	2.3	2.3	25.7
Mexico City, Mexico	T	54	57	61	63	65	64	62	62	61	59	57	55	60
	P	0.2	0.3	0.5	0.7	1.9	4.1	4.5	4.3	4.1	1.6	0.5	0.3	23.0
Moscow, USSR	T	14	17	25	39	55	61	66	62	51	40	28	19	40
	P	1.5	1.4	1.1	1.9	2.2	2.9	3.0	2.9	1.9	2.7	1.7	1.6	24.8
Oslo, Norway	T	24	25	31	41	51	60	63	60	52	42	33	26	42
	P	1.7	1.3	1.4	1.6	1.8	2.4	2.9	3.8	2.5	2.9	2.3	2.3	26.9
Paris, France	T	37	39	43	49	56	62	65	64	59	50	43	38	50
	P	1.5	1.3	1.5	1.7	2.0	2.1	2.1	2.0	2.0	2.2	2.0	1.9	22.3
Port Elizabeth, S.A.	T	70	71	68	66	62	59	58	59	60	63	65	69	64
	P	1.2	1.3	1.9	1.8	2.4	1.8	1.9	2.0	2.3	2.2	2.2	1.7	22.7
Rio de Janeiro, Brazil	T	78	78	77	75	72	70	69	70	70	71	74	76	73
	P	4.9	4.8	5.1	4.2	3.1	2.1	1.6	1.7	2.6	3.1	4.1	5.6	42.6
Rome, Italy	T	45	47	51	57	64	71	76	75	69	62	53	47	60
	P	3.3	2.9	2.0	2.0	1.9	0.7	0.4	0.7	2.8	4.3	4.4	4.1	29.5
Shanghai, P.R.C.	T	38	39	46	56	66	73	81	81	73	63	53	42	59
	P	1.9	2.4	3.3	3.6	3.8	7.0	5.8	5.5	5.2	2.9	2.1	1.5	45.0

		J	F	M	A	M	J	J	A	S	O	N	D	Annual
Sydney, Australia	T	72	71	69	65	59	55	53	55	59	64	67	70	63
	P	3.5	4.0	5.0	5.3	5.0	4.6	4.6	3.0	2.9	2.8	2.9	2.9	46.5
Stockholm, Sweden	T	27	26	30	38	48	57	62	59	53	43	35	29	42
	P	1.5	1.1	1.1	1.5	1.6	1.9	2.8	3.1	2.1	2.1	1.9	1.9	22.4
Tokyo, Japan	T	39	39	45	55	62	70	76	79	73	61	51	42	57
	P	1.9	2.9	4.2	5.3	5.8	6.5	5.6	6.0	9.2	8.2	3.8	2.2	61.6
Vienna, Austria	T	28	32	39	49	58	64	67	66	59	49	38	31	48
	P	1.5	1.4	1.8	2.0	2.8	2.7	3.0	2.7	2.0	2.0	1.9	1.8	25.6

Sources: *Climates of the World*, U.S. Government Printing Office; W. G. Kendrew, *Climates of Continents*, Oxford University Press.

APPENDIX III
Weather and Climatic Information Sources

ORGANIZATIONS (ASSOCIATIONS AND SOCIETIES)

Air Pollution Control Association
4400 Fifth Avenue
Pittsburg, Pennsylvania 15213

American Association of State Climatologists
c/o Bernard E. Dethier, Cornell University
Ithaca, New York 14850

American Geophysical Union (AGU)*
2000 Florida Avenue, N.W.
Washington, D.C. 20009

American Meteorological Society (AMS)
45 Beacon Street
Boston, Massachusetts 02108

Canadian Meteorological and Oceanographic Society
151 Slater Street
Ottawa, Ontario, Canada

National Council of Industrial Meteorologists
c/o Don S. Packnett, P.O. Box 5888
Denver, Colorado 80217

National Weather Association (NWA)
4400 Stamp Road
Temple Hills, Maryland 20748

Royal Meteorological Society
James Glaisher House, Grenville Place
Bracknell, Berkshire RG12 1BX, England

Weather Modification Association
P.O. Box 8116
Fresno, California 93727

World Meteorological Organization (WMO)
Case postale No. 5
CH-1211 Geneva 20 Switzerland

---

*Some of the organizations listed here are commonly identified by acronyms.

ORGANIZATIONS*

Bureau of Meteorology
G.P.O. Box 1289K
Melbourne, Victoria 3001, Australia

Bureau of Reclamation (BuRec)
Department of the Interior (DOI)
Washington, D.C. 20240

Council on Environmental Quality (CEQ)
722 Jackson Place
Washington, D.C. 20006

Department of Energy (DOE)
1000 Independence Avenue, S.W.
Washington, D.C. 20585

Environmental Data and Information Services/NOAA (EDIS)
8621 Fenway Road
Bethesda, Maryland 20034

Environmental Management Service
Ottawa, Ontario K1A 0E3, Canada

Environmental Protection Agency (EPA)
401 M Street, S.W.
Washington, D.C. 20460

Federal Aviation Administration (FAA)
Department of Transportation
Washington, D.C. 20591

Federal Emergency Management Agency (FEMA)
1725 I Street
Washington, D.C. 20472

Geological Survey
Department of the Interior
Reston, Virginia 22092

Meteorological Office
London Road
Bracknell, Berkshire RG12 2SZ, England

National Aeronautics and Space Administration (NASA)
400 Maryland Avenue, S.W.
Washington, D.C. 20546

National Center for Atmospheric Research (NCAR)
P.O. Box 3000
Boulder, Colorado 80307

---

*Governmental, except NCAR.

National Climatic Center/NOAA
Federal Building
Asheville, North Carolina 28801

National Earth Satellite Service/NOAA (NESS)
Washington, D.C. 20233

National Hurricane Center/NOAA
1320 South Dixie Highway
Coral Gables, Florida 33146

National Oceanic and Atmospheric Administration (NOAA)
Department of Commerce
Washington, D.C. 20230

National Science Foundation
Washington, D.C. 20550

National Severe Storms Forecast Center/NOAA
Federal Building
Kansas City, Missouri 64106

National Severe Storms Laboratory/NOAA (NSSL)
1313 Halley Circle
Norman, Oklahoma 73069

National Weather Service/NOAA (NWS)
Central Office: 6121 Wayside Drive
                  Rockville, Maryland 20852
Local Offices: See local telephone book

U.S. Department of Agriculture (USDA)
Washington, D.C. 20250

Water Resources Council
2120 L Street
Washington, D.C. 20037

ACTIVITIES AND SOURCES OF INFORMATION IN UNITED STATES

Air pollution
Air Pollution Control Association
Council on Environmental Quality
Department of Energy
Environmental Protection Agency
National Weather Service/NOAA

Certified consulting meteorologists
American Meteorological Society

Climatic data

Agricultural extension agents at state universities
American Association of State Climatologists
Environmental Data and Information Services/NOAA
National Climatic Center/NOAA
State Climatologists

Cloud seeding

American Meteorological Society
Weather Modification Association

Violent weather forecasts and preparedness information

Federal Emergency Management Agency
National Hurricane Center/NOAA
National Severe Storms Forecast Center/NOAA
National Weather Service/NOAA

Weather forecasters and forecasts

American Meteorological Society
Monthly and Seasonal Weather Outlook. (U.S. Government Printing
   Office, Washington, D.C. 20402.)
National Weather Association
National Weather Service/NOAA

Weather information via radio and television

AM Weather (Public Broadcasting System)
NOAA Radio
The Weather Channel (Cable TV)

For information in Australia, Canada, and the United Kingdom contact the national weather services at the addresses given above.

PERIODICALS, NONTECHNICAL

Bulletin of the American Meteorological Society. (See American Meteorological
Society, above.)
Daily Weather Maps. (U.S. Government printing Office, Washington, D.C.
20402.)
EOS. (See American Geophysical Union, above.)
Monthly and Seasonal Weather Outlook. ((U.S. Government Printing Office,
Washington, D.C. 20402.)
Science News. (1719 N Street N.W., Washington, D.C. 20036.)
Weather. (See Royal Meteorological Society, above.)
Weatherwise. (Heldref Publications, 4000 Albemarle Street N.W., Washington,
D.C. 20016.)
Weekly Weather and Crop Bulletin. (U.S. Department of Agriculture,
Washington, D.C. 20250.)
WMO Bulletin. (See World Meteorological Organization, above.)

Additional Reading

Chapters 1–7

Battan, L. J., *Fundamentals of Meteorology*. Englewood Cliffs, N.J.: Prentice-Hall, 1979.

Byers, H. R., *General Meteorology*, 4th ed.* New York: McGraw-Hill, 1974.

Climate Research Board, *Carbon Dioxide and Climate: A Scientific Assessment*. Washington D.C.: U.S. National Academy of Sciences, 1979.

Hare, F. K., and M. K. Thomas, *Climate Canada*. New York: Wiley, 1974.

Hess, W. N., ed., *Weather and Climate Modification*. New York: Wiley, 1974.

Mather, J. R., *Climatology: Fundamentals and Applications*. New York: McGraw-Hill, 1974.

Maunder, W. J., *The Value of Weather*. New York: Barnes & Noble, 1970.

Schaefer, V. J., and J. Day, *A Field Guide to the Atmosphere*. Boston: Houghton Mifflin, 1981.

Scott, D., ed., *Luke Howard*. York, England: William Sessions, 1976. (Luke Howard's correspondence with Goethe.)

Trewartha, G. T., and L. H. Horn, *An Introduction to Climate*, 5th ed. New York: McGraw-Hill, 1980.

Wallace, J. J., and P. V. Hobbs, *Atmospheric Science, An Introductory Survey*.* New York: Academic Press, 1977.

Chapter 8

Climate Research Board, *Carbon Dioxide and Climate: A Scientific Assessment*. Washington, D.C.: U.S. National Academy of Sciences, 1979.

Eldridge, F.R., *Wind Machines*, 2nd ed. New York: Van Nostrand, 1980.

Geophysics Research Board, *Energy and Climate*. Washington, D.C.: U.S. National Academy of Sciences, 1977.

Golde, R. H., *Lightning Protection*. London: Edward Arnold, 1973.

Halacy, D. S., Jr., *Earth, Water, Wind and Sun: Our Energy Alternatives*. New York: Harper & Row, 1977.

Manabe, S., and R. T. Wetherald, "On the Distribution of Climate Change Resulting from an Increase of CO_2 Content of the Atmosphere," *Journal of Atmospheric Sciences*, vol. 37, January 1980. (A technical article.)

Thorndike, E. H., *Energy and Environment: A Primer for Scientists and Engineers*. Reading, Mass.: Addison-Wesley, 1976.

---

*Advanced introductory textbooks for readers who have studied calculus.

Chapter 9

Board on Agricultural and Renewable Resources, *Climate and Food*. Washington, D.C.: U.S. National Academy of Sciences, 1976.

Critchfield, H. J., *General Climatology*, 3rd ed. Englewood Cliffs, N.J.: Prentice-Hall, 1974.

Mather, J. R., *Climatology: Fundamentals and Applications*. New York: McGraw-Hill, 1974.

Oliver, J. E., *Climate and Man's Environment*. New York: Wiley, 1973.

Rosenberg, N. J., *Microclimate: The Biological Environment*. New York: Wiley, 1974.

Weekly Weather and Crop Bulletin, Agricultural Weather Facility, U.S. Department of Agriculture, South Building, Washington, D.C. 20250. (A summary of each week's weather, drought indices, and monthly precipitation and temperature outlooks for the following month. Emphasis is on the United States, but monthly data is given for many countries.)

Chapter 10

Aviation Weather. Washington, D.C.: U.S. Government Printing Office, 1975.

Kotsch, W. J., *Weather for the Mariner*, 2nd ed. Annapolis, Md.: U.S. Naval Institute Press, 1977.

McCollam, J., *The Yachtman's Weather Manual*. New York: Dodd, Mead, 1973.

Meteorology for Mariners, Meteorological Office Publication No. 895, 3rd ed. London: Her Majesty's Stationery Office, 1978.

Motte, R., *Weather Routing of Ships*. London: Heinemann, 1972.

Pickard, G. L., *Descriptive Physical Oceanography*. Elmsford, N.Y.: Pergamon Press, 1979.

Riehl, H., *Introduction to the Atmosphere*, 3rd ed. New York: McGraw-Hill, 1978.

Silverman, B. A., and A. I. Weinstein, "Fog," Chapter 9 in *Weather and Climate Modification*, W. N. Hess, ed. New York: Wiley, 1974.

Chapter 11

Hollander, J. L., and S. Y. Yeostros, "The Effect of Simultaneous Variations of Humidity and Barometric Pressure on Arthritis," *Bulletin of the Americun Meteorological Society*, vol. 44, August 1963.

Oliver, J. E., *Climate and Man's Environment*. New York: Wiley, 1973.

Persinger, M.A., *The Weather Matrix and Human Behavior*. New York: Praeger, 1980.

Petersen, W. F., *Lincoln-Douglas: The Weather as Destiny*. Springfield, Ill.: C. C. Thomas, 1943.

Reifsynder, W. E., *Weathering the Wilderness*. New York: Scribner's, 1980.

Rosen, S., *Weathering: How the Atmosphere Conditions Your Body, Your Mind, Your Moods—and Your Health*. New York: M. Evans, 1979.

Sargent, F., II, and S. W. Tromp, *A Survey of Human Biometeorology*, Technical Note No. 65. Geneva, Switzerland: World Meteorological Organization, 1964.

Steadman, R. G., "Indices of Windchill of Clothed Persons." *Journal of Applied Meteorology*, vol. 10, August 1971. (A technical article.)

Sulman, F.G., *Health, Weather and Climate*. White Plains, N.Y.: S. Karger, 1976.

Weihe, W. H., "Climate, Health and Disease." *Proceedings of the World Climate Conference*," Report No. 537. Geneva, Switzerland: World Meteorological Organization, 1979.

Young, K. C., "The Influence of Environmental Parameters on Heat Stress During Exercise," *Journal of Applied Meteorology*, vol. 18, July 1979. (A technical article.)

Chapter 12

Aronin, J. E., *Climate and Architecture*. New York: Reinhold, 1953.

Building Research Advisory Board, *Weather and Building Industry*, Proceedings of B.R.A.B. Conference, Report No. 1. Washington, D.C.: U.S. National Academy of Sciences, 1950.

Critchfield, H. J., *General Climatology*, 3rd ed. Englewood Cliffs, N.J.: Prentice-Hall, 1974.

Evans, M., *Housing, Climate, and Comfort*. London: The Architectural Press, 1980.

Golde, R. H., *Lightning Protection*. London: Edward Arnold, 1973.

Green, K. W., "Climate and Architecture," *Environmental Data and Information Service*, vol. 10, September 1979, pp. 6–10.

Housing and Home Finance Agency, *Application of Climatic Data to Home Design*. Washington, D.C.: U.S. Government Printing Office, 1954.

Loftness, V., "Climate and Architecture," *Weatherwise*, vol. 31, December 1978, pp. 212–217.

Mather, J. R., *Climatology: Fundamentals and Applications*. New York: McGraw-Hill, 1974.

Olgyay, V. G., *Design with Climate: Bioclimatic Approach to Architectural Regionalism*. Princeton, N.J.: Princeton University Press, 1963.

Oliver, J. E., *Climate and Man's Environment*. New York: Wiley, 1973.

Chapter 13

Bonacina, L. C. W., "Landscape Meteorology and Its Reflection in Art and Literature," *Quarterly Journal of the Royal Meteorological Society*, vol. 65, 1939.

Clark, K., *Landscape into Art*. London: John Murray, 1949.

Clifford, F. A., "James Gillray's 'Weather' Etchings," *Bulletin of American Meteorological Society*, vol. 59, August 1978.

Greenler, R., *Rainbows, Halos, and Glories*. London: Cambridge University Press, 1980.

Heuer, K., *Thunder, Singing Sands and Other Wonders*. New York: Dodd, Mead, 1981.

Humpheries, W. J., *Ways of the Weather*. Lancaster, Pa.: Jacques Cattell, 1942.

Lamb, H. H., "Climatic History and the Future," vol. 2 of *Climate: Present, Past and Future*. London: Methuen & Co., Ltd., 1977.

Le Roy Ladurie, E., *Times of Feast, Times of Famine: A History of Climate Since the Year 1000* (translated by Barbara Bray). New York: Doubleday, 1971.

Salanave, L.E., *Lightning and Its Spectrum*. Tucson: University of Arizona Press, 1980.

Sloane, E., *For Spacious Skies*. New York: Funk & Wagnalls, 1978.

Thornes, J. E., "The Weather Dating of John Constable's Cloud Studies," *Weather*, vol. 34, August 1979.

Wagner, A. J., "More Music for Weather Watchers," *Weatherwise*, vol. 31, October 1978.

Wagner, A. J., "Music to Watch Weather By," *Weatherwise*, vol. 25, August 1972.

Index